Write To Meow
2017

Edited by Victoria L. Scott

Grey Wolfe Publishing, LLC
145 East Fourteen Mile Road
Clawson, MI 48017
www.GreyWolfePublishing.com

© 2018 Grey Wolfe Publishing, LLC
Published by Grey Wolfe Publishing, LLC
www.GreyWolfePublishing.com
All Rights Reserved

Print ISBN: 978-1628281996
E-book ISBN: 978-1628282023
Library of Congress Control Number: 2018936052

Grey Wolfe Publishing LLC
Ní bóna na coróin

Write To Meow
2017

Edited by Victoria L. Scott

Dedication

We humbly dedicate this book to the cat; young ones, old ones, big ones, small ones, and all the exotics suffering in shelters, waiting for their "furever" homes or languishing in inappropriate housing conditions.

Perhaps through the writing contained in these pages, more humans will come to understand the unconditional love and selfless devotion you bring to their lives, and will open their hearts and homes to you.

No more homeless cats, no more abused or neglected big cats, this is our prayer for you today and always!

Acknowledgements

We would like to send out a special **Thank You** to all of the fine authors who submitted their work for this book. It is because of your dedication to cats, as well as the writing craft, that we have been able to produce such a spectacular tribute to our furry friends!

We also want to thank the good people of **Big Cat Rescue** who fight tirelessly day after day to make sure that big cats and exotic felines find all the love, medical care, and comfort they deserve!

And finally, we want to thank **you**, the person who purchased this book and is about to read it. Because of your interest in cats, or perhaps because of the relationship you have with one of the authors, big cats will be saved, cared for, and find a special place in a loving sanctuary!

Table of Contents

A Chat Noir	David Groveman	1
Animal Eyes	Edward Ahern	9
Animal Lover	Ryan R. Ennis	10
A Walk On The Beach	David Rochon	19
Black Jack	Mark Hudson	23
Blue Cat	Gareth Writer-Davies	24
Captain Kai	Leslie Soule	25
Cat's Eyes	Sarah M. Lewis	26
Cats	A.J. Huffman	27
Feline Fire Brigade	A.J. Huffman	28
Home for Wayward Cats	A.J. Huffman	29
I Am A Cat	Mark Hudson	30
Kato's Grand Adventure	Jasmine and Jim Tritten	31
Miss Kitty's French Toast	Carol Hanson	58
Morning After Ballet	Sarah Milne Das	62
Oswald, The Magnificent Protector of Potted Plants	Sarah M. Lewis	68
Pizazz	Elisabeth Ward	76
Rescue	Dexter Morales	82
Resistance Is Futile	Patricia Walkow	83
The Cat Got Paddled	A.J. Huffman	88
The Cat That Changed My Life	Susan P. Blevins	89
The Cat	A. Elizabeth Herting	92
The Christmas Cat Art Show	Mark Hudson	97
The Katz' Kittens	Sherry Williams	101
The Tell-Tale Tail	Claudia R. Coleman	119
Tiger	Patricia Walkow	122
Traveling Tales	Beth Clegg	126

Venus the Calico Coat   Mark Hudson   133
Wally   Roseanne Trost   134
Wildcat   C.R. Beideman   138

A Chat Noir
David Groveman

It was the kind of night where I wanted nothing more than to curl up into a ball and forget about the troubles of this lonely world. A night with dark clouds, so heavy they can't decide if they want to rain or just fall from the sky.

I was still recovering from my part in the Calico Caper, and I knew better. Like most men who know better, I decided to throw caution to the wind and head out anyway. My roommate was away, and I figured if that great big clumsy oaf was having a good time, why shouldn't I?

Do you know that feeling you get when you know you're making the wrong call? That twisting sensation in the pit of your gut that makes you feel like you're about to cough up a hairball? Well, I got that feeling as I left the apartment.

I used the fire escape. I always used the fire escape, as my roommate, bless his sweet dimwitted heart, never remembered to make me a key. Had I used the front door I never would have seen her, but that's just the way fate is.

She was the hottest piece of tail I'd ever laid my eyes on. The kind of girl that mothers worry their sons will get mixed up with and warn them about. Unluckily, for me anyway, I never knew my mother. The dame was wrapped snug in soft white fur and had a pink little nose peeking out beneath her deep green eyes.

She was coming out of the apartment next door. A classier joint than the one my roommate and I shared, but as I was drastically behind on my half of the rent, who was I to complain. She'd left the apartment and stopped by the street, seeming unsure of where to go and what to do. I could'a given her a few suggestions, but instead, I minded my manners.

"What's a dame like you doing out on a night like this?"

She turned and held me in the gaze of her emerald green eyes, stopping me in my tracks. I've always been a sucker for dames, but I'd never felt so naked in my entire life.

"I'm not interested."

I heard what she said, but her eyes had said something entirely different. "I wasn't offering, but maybe I should."

"Didn't your mother tell you girls like me were trouble?"

"Didn't know my mother. Perhaps you should give me some instruction on the subject?" I was as smitten as a schoolboy and didn't know the half of the trouble I was really in." How about you and I get to know one another over drinks?"

She was ready to refuse when a sound from her apartment made her jump like a flock of sparrows the second after a cat pounces. "Let's go!"

I was a fool for following her but, follow her I did.

****

She wanted to go somewhere but didn't know the neighborhood, so I took her to a joint behind the Old Presbyterian Church. It wasn't the kind of place where a purebred broad like her would normally spend her evenings, but I wasn't exactly the breed of Tom to tell her she'd made a mistake in going out with me in the first place.

The owner of the establishment nodded to me, "What'll it be, Jasper?"

"The usual," I said trailing off to give her time to make an order.

She took the hint like this was a game she'd played before." Make that two and see if you can give us a little privacy."

She gave him a wink that made me feel fuller of myself than a float at Macy's on Thanksgiving, but she gave me a cool glare that quickly rained out my parade. We made our way to a quiet corner and waited for our drinks while I felt the searing envy of every other guy in the room. If things turned ugly, which I was sure they would, it wouldn't end well for me.

"So, Jasper, what's a hep cat like you do for a living?"

"This and that," I answered vaguely. I didn't need her to know that I was as down on my luck as I was. Besides, if this dame said she needed me to be a trained circus lion you could bet your last dime that I was perfect for the role. "What about you, Miss?"

She rolled her eyes as if annoyed to play this game. "My name is Clara, and I'm fortunate to not have to work for a living."

Classy dame with fur like that, I should have known she was born with a silver spoon. I was already over my head and drowning fast, so I cut to the chase. "So, what's a slinky little minx like you going out with a ginger-haired shlub like me?"

Her eyes narrowed again, but not with anger. The deep green orbs filled with laughter as she sized me up for the fifteenth time that night. "You're cute, in a rumpled and dirty kind of way, you know that?"

"Not at all, but I'll let you go on at length if you must."

She laughed, and I knew, even without my mother telling me, that I was in far too deep. To call it love would be trite and melodramatic but there were several other feelings she inspired in me that I wouldn't want to share with my confessor. "Jasper, I like you, you're funnier than most men, and I haven't laughed in a long time."

My luck hadn't been this good in years, so I decided to press it before it changed. "Why don't we go back to my place? My roommate is out, and I'm sure we can continue to find ways to amuse ourselves." I'd like to think she would've said yes, had she had the chance, but I'll never know for sure.

In that moment, there was a yowl from the front and a voice like a slow roll of thunder." Where is she?"

****

In short, I was a dead. To make the same story longer, I didn't have much longer to live. The gent at the door was all in black, as clean and sleek as Clara and twice as dangerous. I wasn't scared of him, of course; I was terrified.

"Calm down, Max." Clara spoke to the figure in the doorway." I'm right here." Clara stood up and walked towards him, oozing sex in a way that made our previous flirtations seem like a schoolyard folly.

"Who's your friend?" Max asked, prowling up to me in a way that was meant to make me feel small and afraid.

Clara stepped back." He's no friend, just a poor stiff trying to make a girl smile on a rainy night."

"A funny guy, eh?" Max glared at me, his eyes shining yellow and fierce. "Tell me a joke, funny guy."

I cleared my throat. "Have you heard the one about the fella who bought another guy a drink to show it had all been a misunderstanding?"

"As a matter of fact, I have," Max spoke in his deep growling voice making the hairs on my neck and back stand on edge. "I believe the guy broke that fella's neck to show how deeply he understood."

Clara stood between us." Max, no!"

Max simply shouldered her away and leapt at me like he was a panther and I was whatever it was that panthers ate. I darted away, avoiding his first lunge by a whisker. He had me on size, speed and fighting prowess, that was plain to see, but I had him on intuition and gumption. I bolted like a rabbit from a trap and hoped against hope that my friend wasn't asleep.

Max was after me in a flash, with the distance between us vanishing faster than a snowball in Hell. It was my neighborhood, and that small advantage kept my hide in one piece, for now. I slid through an alley and hopped through several gardens, Max at my heels at every turn. I was hanging on to a whisker of a chance and cursing my lack of any particular physical fitness regimen.

I made my way up a flight of steps, and across a dark porch, sure I'd feel Max grabbing from behind when a light came on, and a door flew open. I was just on the other side of the wash of bright white light, but Max was stunned and blinded by it for an instant.

My friend reached down and grabbed him up in her firm grip. "What a big kitty-witty," Mrs. Pollander cooed at the bewildered muscular black cat. "Would you like some yum yums?" He was too shocked or well-mannered to resist, either way, I was glad that Max wouldn't stoop to scratch old ladies.

She carried him away, and I knew that poor Max had an evening of stale kibble, a cold bath and maybe even a cute little sweater ahead of him. It was a cruel trick, but I didn't care so long as it kept me in one piece. I made my way back to the dumpster behind the church.

Clara was as surprised as I was to see me walking back, not too much the worse for wear. "How did you…" She began, but I stopped her with a wink.

"Looks like Max didn't know about Mrs. Pollander and her penchant for adopting strays. Now, how about you and I find something to laugh about."

****

Clara and I didn't last. I never thought we would, her being a purebred princess and me a ginger tabby, but we had fun while it lasted. I returned to find my roommate asleep in his bed and a fresh tin of tuna waiting for me.

I thanked him and nudged him to give me some room beneath the covers. After all, I'd had a hard night and deserved it.

After that night I didn't see Clara ever again though I think I spied Max in the window of Mrs. Pollander's wearing a bonnet and cute little booties. I supposed it was for the best that I never saw her again. I was a confirmed bachelor, and I could never make a classy broad like Clara happy for long. Besides, it was far more excitement than an old cat like me needed, and I vowed to not go chasing any more dames.

That vow didn't last long, but they never do...

Animal Eyes
For Barbara the catwoman
Edward Ahern

Are we less or more human
When we watch the world
Through animal eyes?

When we react to strangers
Through the growls or purrs
Of the four legged?

When we ensure that
The hair lined mammal
Is fed before us?

Do we bond with fellow men
Based on association with dogs
Or cohabitation with cats?

Are we subspecies hominids
Living for the company
Of the inarticulate?

Probably.

But I have spent forty years
Observing life through animals' eyes
And feel better for it.

Animal Lover
Ryan R. Ennis

Growing up in a Dutch colonial with two affectionate and protective Bouvier des Flanders, in Michigan's thumb area, Mason thought his destiny was to always be a dog lover. That notion changed one September morning during his sophomore year. On the ride home from the Saturday Farmer's Market, Mason saw a man holding a cat over a winding creek. What was the guy going to do with it? Throw the poor thing in? Try to drown it? The scene tore at Mason's heart.

Estimating the creek to be about a hundred yards away, Mason believed he could save the animal before it was too late." Dad, stop!" he yelled, pointing to the gravel shoulder of the country road.

Hitting the brakes, his dad pulled the Chrysler minivan over." What the hell, Mason? What's the matter? You sick or something?"

Without responding, he jumped out of the van, not bothering to shut the door. Waving his arms, he screamed, "Hey, Mister! Please—please don't do that! Don't hurt that cat!" In excellent physical shape, he ran effortlessly as muddy water shot up from the rain-saturated field, soaking his tennis shoes and jeans.

Seeing six-foot-three Mason heading toward him, the much shorter man dropped the cat on the grass. As the man leaped over the creek, his sports cap fell off his head and landed in the water. Without pausing to retrieve the hat, the bald stranger headed up a small hill, then disappeared into a cluster of trees.

Carefully, Mason picked up the orange-and-white-striped cat, inspecting it to see if it was hurt anywhere. Appearing unharmed, the cat purred in his arms. As he cuddled it like a baby, it nuzzled the shoulder of his fleece jacket." You're so beautiful—handsome," Mason told it, unsure if it was a boy or a girl.

Red-faced and gasping for breath, his father caught up with him, saying, "Son, you almost made lose me control of the car." His father looked down and pointed to his muddy boots." And you made a mess of these."

Mason set the cat on his shoulder, petting its soft back." Can I keep it?"

His father shook his head.

"At least until we find out if it belongs to anyone other than that crazy guy..."

Rubbing his forehead, his father was silent for a moment, then said, "Okay—but if no one claims the cat in a month, I'll have to hand it over to the Humane Society. Your mom won't put up with two dogs and a cat under the same roof for very long."

To their surprise, his mom said she didn't mind the new addition. She even helped make the missing-cat flyers that Mason and his dad posted around town and the neighboring communities.

Concerned about the animal's health, he convinced his dad to take the cat to the vet, who told them it was a neutered male. Calling the cat "Burr-boy"—because that might've been the animal's fate in that cold creek—Mason kept the feline in his bedroom, away from the cat-skeptical dogs. With balls of yarn and stuffed toys, he spent many evenings playing with the animal. Often, his red-haired and freckle-faced girlfriend, Laurie, joined him.

"Cats are so cool," he told her, watching Burr-boy bat his paw at the pretend stuffed mouse on the floor and knock it across the imitation-wood laminate." I like how Burr-boy can be with me without being all over me. When one of those beefy Bouviers tries to get on my lap, I feel suffocated."

Reclining with Mason against a headboard of pillows, she combed her piano fingers through his fine sandy hair." And I like how his fur is as soft as your hair."

And what I like even better, he thought, *is that the cat seems to bring us closer together.* Their month-long relationship still had its awkward moments. Without a lot in common—he enjoyed long hikes in the woods; she preferred being indoors—they struggled at times to have a conversation. At their disposal for discussion was gossip about mutual friends, or the brewing scandal concerning the school principal's affair with one of their teachers and... yet they exhausted those topics within minutes. Now, when they were alone, Burr-boy relieved the pressure of what to do, what to say.

As his attachment to the feline grew, so did his gratitude that no one ever contacted his parents about a lost cat. After school, he often went with Laurie to the public library to read and check out cat care books while she studied. (He found he did his best studying on his bed with his back against a stack of pillows and Burr-boy curled up on his lap.)

In a book entitled *How to Keep Your Kitty Meowing* were several fun exercise games for cats. One game called Catching the Light became Burr-boy's favorite. In his darkened bedroom, laughing so hard that his stomach hurt, he shined a flashlight around and watched the cat jump on the bed, the desk chair, the desk, the clothes hamper in his attempt to paw at the light. In order not to frustrate Burr-boy too much, Mason allowed him to actually "catch" the light once in a while. Feeling guilty about neglecting Duke and Duchess, the dogs, he changed his weekend plans to devote more attention to them. Instead of going with their friends to the Port Huron Factory Shops, a discount outlet, he went on walks with Laurie and the dogs to the nearby park. In the area designated as a dog run, they unleashed the Bouviers and threw softballs for the animals to fetch. The game lasted about thirty minutes until Duke and Duchess flopped down in front of the bench on which he and Laurie sat. To quench their thirst, the dogs drank the water in a rectangular plastic container set at their feet.

It was on a late-October afternoon at the park that Laurie told him the upsetting news:

"Mason," she said, looking into his eyes, "I've been wondering about *us*." She brushed her long straight hair back behind her ears." I mean we're sorta 'going out,' but it doesn't really feel like it. It kinda feels like we're connecting more as friends."

Though he somewhat agreed with what she said—going out for three months and no make-out sessions, only awkward kisses—her revelation stunned him. Then angered him, heating his face up like a hot poker. This skinny backstabber was actually rejecting him. Did she really think she could find something better, with her pug-like nose and pointed chin like a witch, with her outdated and baggy-fitting clothes looking like hand-me-downs? She was nothing so special that she could reject him first. And he hadn't even wanted to date her in the first place, got pushed into it by their mutual friends, Jay and Tina. Trying to fit in, to be "cool," he wanted to be in a relationship like the rest of his friends.

His immaturity getting the best of him, he shook his head, flaring, "Look, if you weren't interested, you should've said it two months ago. Why play games and waste time?"

As he stood up and hopped over the dogs, she reached for his hand, but he backed far enough away that she couldn't touch him." Sorry," she said, "I like you—I really do. At first, I thought maybe a little more than just *like*.

Don't be upset. What's wrong with being friends?"

"Nothin'—I guess," he said with bitterness, pulling the dogs up with their leashes." I gotta go." He tugged gently at each dog's leash until Duke and Duchess were standing. With the dogs leading the way, he hurried out of the park.

"Hey!" she called after him." What about the container you brought? What do you want me to do with it?"

"Stick your head in it!" he yelled. He crossed the gravel parking lot, then the road to the dirt path on the other side, grateful for the breeze cooling his face. Jogging along that path, he reached his house in about fifteen minutes. On the front porch, the dogs bent their heads, as trained, so that he could easily unleash them.

Once inside, the dogs headed straight for their rugs in the den. Mason was about to head upstairs, but his mom's frantic voice drew him into the kitchen. Entering the room, he discovered her cries were coming through the fully-opened French doors in the dining area. He followed it outside, onto the deck, where he saw his mother standing on the edge of the steps, shaking a cat-treats bag and calling across the yard, "Here, Burr-boy. Here, baby. Come home, Burr-boy. Got a treat for you."

"Mom," he said excitedly, "what's happened? Where's Burr-boy?"

Turning to face him, she let out a loud sigh. Clutching the treats bag against the skirt of her purple dress– (his father's favorite because it complemented her blue-black hair so well), she explained, "Oh, honey, since you were gone with the dogs, I made the mistake of bringing Burr-boy downstairs. He's been cooped up in your room so much." She took a deep breath." He was having a great time exploring the kitchen, finding the treats I left around. For just a moment, I had the doors open, to check out the weather, when Burr-boy bolted past me and scurried away, into the woods." She patted him on the shoulder." Don't get upset, Mason. I'm sure he'll be back before nightfall. He knows he has a good home here."

Overcome with worry, he ran past his mom, down the sloping lawn, into the woods. For what seemed like hours, he jogged, then walked along the overgrown paths crisscrossing the half square mile of forest. Thorny plants and sharp twigs tore at his pant legs. Frequently, he paused to crouch and stick his head through the low tree branches, looking and calling for Burr-boy. Sweat drenched his hooded sweatshirt and plastered his hair across his forehead. His leg muscles ached; his head reeled from exhaustion. Not seeing Burr-boy anywhere, he gave up and went home.

He collapsed into a supine position on the deck, staring at the sky, with his hands folded underneath his head. He observed quick-moving gray clouds, threatening to pour rain, settle overhead. *Poor Burr-boy!* He thought, his eyes turning tearful. *Two months ago, I rescued you from that crazy guy, and now you're gone. All alone in the woods. I hope you're taking cover wherever you are, in case a storm erupts. And most of all, I hope you come back to me.*

The sound of his mother's high heels smacking across the wood planks interrupted Mason's thoughts. Rolling onto his side, he saw that she was approaching with the cordless phone in her hands, her fingers covering the handset's transmitter, as if she didn't want whoever was on the other end to hear them. He sat up, crossing his legs Indian-style.

"Any luck finding Burr-boy?" his mom asked, her brow creased with concern.

Mason shook his head.

"Honey, Laurie's on the phone. She says she really needs to talk to you—that it's important. I know you're pretty upset right now. Do you feel up to talking to her?"

He pulled at his chin, thinking, *What to do? What to say?*

Just then, Burr-boy hopped through the railing onto the deck. As if to answer Mason's questions, another cat, tiger-striped with a mixture of sandy and gray tones, followed Burr-boy. The felines made their way toward him but stopped at his feet. They stared at him, as if they, too, wondered what he would do and say.

"Oh, honey, I told you Burr-boy would come home," his mother said." And look, he's got a friend with him."

Mason stretched his arm until his mom set the phone in his hand. Then, putting the receiver to his ear, he said, "Hello, Laurie... Yes, we need to talk. Long story—but the day got a lot worse after I ran off at the park. Can I call you back in a while? I'll explain more then. Probably in about an hour. Okay?" However, she kept him on the phone, clearly not ready to hang up until he uttered, "No worries, Laurie. I'm the one who should be sorry..." After a brief pause, he asked, "Hey, you want to just come by in an hour? I have something to show you—a surprise." She tried asking him a question about it, but he cut her off with some hints: "Okay, what does every animal and human need? And I'm not talking about water, food, air, or shelter. Don't answer now—think about it. Have to go for now. See you soon," he added, then abruptly ended the call to tend to Burr-boy and his new friend.

A Walk On The Beach
David Rochon

Gary and his cat Max strolled side by side along a deserted beach. The waves lapped at their feet, and the setting sun reflected fire in Max's yellow eyes.

"Gary?"

"Yeah, Max?"

"You've always been real good to me. I just wanted to, you know, say thanks. Not everyone likes cats you know. People aren't always nice like you."

"Like Jenny, you mean."

Max looked up at Gary, a knowing smile danced in his burning eyes.

"Jenny didn't dislike cats. Not really. She was just allergic is all. Anyway, she left over a year ago, so..."

"Was your dad allergic too?" Max asked.

Gary sighed, "Dad was one of those guys who didn't think it was masculine for a man to have a cat for a pet."

"What was it he used to always say?" Max asked, "The only thing a cat is good for is--"

"—target practice," Gary finished.

"I'm just glad you didn't turn out like him," Max said.

"Dad died when you were just a kitten. I'm surprised you even remember him. I'm sorry if he was ever mean to you."

They walked on in silence for a while, letting the sounds of the surf and the seagulls wash over them. After a while Gary said, "Max, can I ask you something?"

"Sure thing, buddy," Max replied.

Gary said, "Why can you talk now?"

"You don't remember?" Max said.

Gary stopped walking and shook his head no. He crouched down and looked at Max expectantly. Max shook some sand from his coat before plopping down to begin bathing himself. Gary waited. After a while, Max said, "I'm not really here."

"I don't understand," Gary said.

Max looked up from his bath and said, "You were running to answer the phone. You were wearing socks, which did not agree with the tile floor in the kitchen. You slipped and hit your head on the counter."

An angry pain screamed across Gary's temple as the memory of the fall came back to him. His crouched position gave way to a seated one.

"It's bad, isn't it?"

Max nodded a solemn yes. They sat in silence for a few minutes while Gary rubbed his head and Max continued to lick himself.

"You should know," Max said, "that when the cat food runs out, I'm going to start eating your body. I hope you understand that it's nothing personal."

"I'd like to think that someone would come to check on me before it comes to that," Gary said.

Max stopped fussing with his fur and looked up with huge sad eyes. "Oh, Gary... we both know that's not going to happen."

Gary stood up and stared at what was left of the sunset. Stars began to wink into existence in the darkening sky above. Tears filled Gary's eyes.

"I don't want to die."

"I know you don't, buddy," Max said.

"Is this... .is this heaven?" Gary asked.

Max looked up and down the beach." I don't think so," he said, "I'd expect heaven to be more populated."

"Is there a heaven?" Gary asked, tears streaming down his cheeks.

Max stood up and gave a cat's best approximation of a shrug.

"What do I do now?" Gary asked.

"Keep walking I suppose," said Max.

The sun had completely disappeared behind the ocean. Gary and Max continued their stroll down the beach, the waves lapping at their feet.

Black Jack
Mark Hudson

*(from an article; by Sara McCormake) 2010
from the internet England)*

Jack was a black cat, a Rotherham muggy,
roaming the streets on a night so foggy.
Scrambling along a metal fence,
he got stuck on the pike, with pain so intense.
Onto the spike, his leg got impaled,
to cross the fence, he had failed.
Some firefighters came and rushed him to the vet,
and he got there in time to have his legs reset.
His black cat fur had to be given a shave.
But he has eight lives, one short of the grave.
Around his neck is a plastic cone,
In other words, "Leave that wound alone!"
He ended up having a successful operation,
but he was an English internet sensation.

Blue Cat
Gareth Writer-Davies

I have yet to decide
(motive)

but
I am wearing your tom-coat

the house
smells

I can taste
mouse upon my tongue

you open
a can of tuna

the rug
grows claws beneath my feet

only birds
sing to their mates

Captain Kai
Leslie Soule

She sits up in the crow's nest/cat tree
A tortoiseshell/calico
With a stubby foot
And an umbilical hernia
She's the sweetest captain
On the high seas –
Captain Kai!
I bought her a Halloween costume that she hates,
But it made her look so cute –
Like a pirate captain –
Captain Kai!
She headbutts her momma for attention now,
But she was the shelter's prisoner
For a long two years
Until she was set free –
Captain Kai!
She jumps with three good legs, up leaps and bounds!
She sits in the sun
And surveys everything around!
Captain Kai! Captain Kai! Captain Kai!

Cat's Eyes
Sarah M. Lewis

I see through the eyes of the Tabby,
streaking through the fields,
slapping at the snake slithering through the grass,
racing up the tree
chasing the chittering squirrel.

I see through the eyes of the Siamese,
gold light and green leaves,
the whir of movement,
the hummingbird hovers,
I pause before I pounce.

I see through the eyes of the Calico,
endless cold gray corridors,
filled with ankles attached to people.
The Angel of Death floats by.
He sees me looking out at him.

Faces filled with pity
blur before me.
Their hands feed me, bathe me.
"Poor old dear.
She isn't really here anymore."

I see through the eyes of cats.

Cats
A.J. Huffman

I am calico.
Giant ball of patchworked fur.
Ya gotta love me.

I am Dragon Li.
Born of Chinese folklore, I
am one smart tabby.

I am Cornish Rex.
Hairless comforter, I love
to decrumb your lap.

I am Egyptian Mau.
Descendant of duck hunters,
I'd rather fetch toys.

I am Siamese.
Social diva, I demand
all your attention.

Feline Fire Brigade
A.J. Huffman

The temple cats are restless,
as if they can feel
the spark in the air.

Smoke signal from villagers
is answered by howling,
a stampede of feet and fur,
as they hurry toward the flames.

Unafraid, they lure fiery tendrils
into calming ash.   The singed
carry the dead back to the healing
hands of their goddess.

Heroic revival rewards them,
but does diminish tally
of lives to eight.

Home for Wayward Cats
A.J. Huffman

The old farmer's field was always full
of cats of various sizes, shades, breeds.
New ones appeared periodically, dropped
off in the wee hours by anonymous cars,
trucks, vans. These unwanted remnant runts
of random litters kept the inbreeding
to a minimum, though some still showed
the hackneyed signs – extra toes, almost feral
distemper. Still, all were welcomed each morning
with pie tins full of milk and food, the first chore
on the farmer's wife's to-do list, the first true
act of kindness I remember witnessing as a child.

I Am A Cat
Mark Hudson

Before class, I got my coffee from the corner café,
and went to the bench on the opposite corner, and sat.
I was sitting in front of an animal hospital that day,
reading a book by Soseki Natsume, I am a Cat.
He's a Japanese author, who lived far away,
and visited London, the place his mission was at.
The book is perspectives of a cat that is a stray,
observing human behavior like analyzing gnats.
I read the introduction, and felt quite okay,
as an ambulance rode by, making such a spat.
A pet owner brought her cat into the vet nigh,
and comforted the creature, giving it a chat.
I guess sirens might even scare a kitten,
but I was serene on the bench where I was sitting.

Kato's Grand Adventure
Jasmine and Jim Tritten

Tori Gets a Kitten

Kato was warm and comfortable snuggled in the tall lady's lap. She wore a fuzzy sweater he could knead. The lady loved to stroke his soft white belly while rocking back and forth in the wooden chair on the porch. The kitten closed his eyes and breathed in the delicious smells coming from the house. He thought, *Maybe she'll open a can of that wonderful food I really like.*

Life was good at this house. Until last night that is. Sister went outside on her own and never came back. Everyone looked for Sister – but she couldn't be found.

The kitten purred loudly and was startled when he heard the loud noises from the driveway. Peeking through one eye, he saw the mud-streaked red box with wheels pull up. Dust flew into the air.

A little girl with two braids got out of the big red box with wheels and ran to the porch. "Hi, Mrs. Taylor. We're here for the two kittens."

The small boy kitten was jostled as Mrs. Taylor got up to greet the young girl." Hello, Tori."

He knew his nap was over and jumped down to the floor and looked at the young girl. He watched another tall lady get out of the red box and walk to the porch.

Mrs. Taylor said, "I'm so sorry, but the little white girl kitten got out last night, and we can't find her. All I have left is this little boy. Every other kitten and the mother have all found new homes."

Tori screeched, "Oh, no! I wanted the little girl. Have you looked everywhere Mrs. Taylor?"

"Yes, Tori, but I'm afraid she's lost somewhere outside. I think she ran off into the woods last evening."

The boy kitten wasn't sure what they were talking about but could sense something was wrong. Maybe they were talking about his sister. *Where is she? Did she go away like everyone else?*

"Mama," said Tori, "I want a little girl kitty of my own. One I can play with and dress up."

Tori's mama looked at her." We'll take this little boy kitten. He'll play with you just the same. Come here Tori, look at him. He's got soft long hair and beautiful striped gray and black markings. His paws look like they've been dipped in a can of white paint."

The kitten looked up at the humans looking at him with their hands moving around and up and down. *I wonder what they're saying?*

"Tori, look at his pale green-colored eyes. They are the same color as our house."

Mrs. Taylor added, "And doesn't he have the cutest little rust-colored nose. And look at his little pink toes."

Tori smiled as she reached down." Mama, look at the long hairs coming out of his ears." The little girl picked him up, and he wiggled until she finally adjusted him to fit in her arms.

The kitten looked up at the smiling freckled face. He sniffed the air and blinked his eyes. *She seems like a nice little girl. I wonder if she'll help me find Sister.* The kitten purred and closed his eyes as she hugged him.

"Oh Mama, I do want to take him home." Tori rocked the kitten back and forth and put her nose right up to his fur. She took in a deep breath and then held him up under his forearms." Mama, I'm going to call him Kato."

A New Home

That first night Kato slept on a pillow right next to Tori's head. He smelled Tori's hair, which had a scent of vanilla. He purred as he kneaded her long hair.

This is sure a nice new home. It's clean and warm and has wonderful new smells. He really liked the warm fish Mama had prepared for dinner. He rolled his head to the side and put his left paw over his eyes. *I'm going to like living here. But, I won't be happy until Sister is here too.* As Kato fell sound asleep, he thought: *I must find her.*

The next morning, Kato opened his eyes and got up. He stretched his front and then his hind legs. He looked at the sleeping girl and meowed. When Tori did not immediately wake up, Kato gently put his paw on her chin.

Tori stirred, stretched, and then got out of bed. She scooped up Kato, and the kitten squirmed until he got comfortable in her arms. Tori walked down the circular staircase holding Kato like a baby – right up against her chest. Something smelled delicious, and there was steam and a crackling sound coming from the top of the stove. Tori's brothers and dad sat around the table eating breakfast. Four big dogs barked outside.

Inside, three cream-colored Siamese cats sat on the kitchen floor. They looked up at Kato in Tori's arms, while squinting their blue eyes. They flicked their long tails back and forth. One of them jumped up onto the center console and then onto a tall black box with doors. It turned around and lay down with both front paws folded under its chest and starred at Kato.

Kato looked up at the Siamese, "How do you like it here?" he asked.

The Siamese cat did not reply. Instead, the cat jumped down from the tall black box, walked out of the room followed by the other two with their tails held high, their hips swaying from side to side.

Kato was completely confused – didn't these cats understand him? *Maybe they just don't want to talk to me.*

After squirming and fussing in Tori's arms, she put him down.

Kato walked over to the window, stood up on his hind legs, moved his black-tipped tail from side to side, and looked out at the large dogs yelping in the yard. Two of the dogs were growling while playing tug-of-war with an old rope. *I sure hope Sister is not out there with those dogs.*

Tori's mama heated up some chicken on the stove and put a bowl of it on the floor for Kato to eat.

Kato thought, *Hmmmmm, good.* When his soft white belly was full, he licked his left paw, then wiped his face with the paw, and looked for a nice place to take a nap.

Before he could settle down, Tori picked him up and ran upstairs.

What's she doing?

Tori dressed him in frilly doll's clothes.

Kato struggled to get out of the dress and run away. *Even if everything is nice at this house; I've got to find Sister. Maybe she'll like playing with this little girl.*

He thought, *I don't want to be in a dress.*

Escape

That afternoon Mama told Tori and her two brothers, "Please go get Kato and bring him with you into the Jeep. We're going to take him to the vet for a checkup."

Tori wrapped Kato into a knit blanket and put him on the back seat, next to her brothers. He quickly untangled his claws from the blanket and jumped up on the back of the seat, high enough to see what was passing by outside. *Maybe we're going to look for Sister?* Kato looked back at the pale green house that was now his home. He saw a pond on his right, and then they crossed a stream, as the red box with wheels, called a Jeep, went down the driveway.

When they reached the main road, Mama got out to open the gate and to check the mail. Tori rolled down the rear window to tell Mama she wanted to go to the store and buy some new dresses for the kitten.

Kato was looking outside and saw something white walking through the bushes. He cried out, "Sister!" With lightning speed, he jumped through the open window and down into the bushes.

Tori and her brothers shrieked. Mama turned to see what the matter was. But all she saw was Kato's dark-tipped tail disappearing into the dark brush and down a gully.

"Kato!" they all shouted. But Kato didn't hear them. Mama, Tori, and her brothers looked at each other with horror as they realized their kitten was gone.

****

The dry brown leaves quivered as something ahead of Kato ran deeper into the forest and towards a gurgling stream. *It must be Sister.* Kato called to his sister, but no one answered. *Where did she go?*

All Kato could hear was gently moving water and the cackling of crows above in the trees. It reminded him of the woods where he lived with his sister and Mrs. Taylor. Kato closed his eyes and purred as he thought how they both used to play in the brush chasing mice, beetles, and small striped lizards. He listened for the sounds of Sister running... but couldn't hear anything.

The sounds of water drew him down into the gully. It was cold and dark as he pushed his way deeper towards the bubbling sounds. When Kato reached the stream, he looked into a small pool of water, where the current barely moved the brown leaves floating on the surface.

Kato saw his own image reflected in the pool, like in a mirror, and reached down to pat the water with his paw. Then he licked his paw. The water was cold and wet. Kato bent forward and lapped up some - splashing drops on his face and whiskers. *Hmmmmm, sure tastes good!*

While walking along the side of the stream holding his tail high, Kato chased wandering bugs and flying insects. Some of the leaves moved, and he spotted a mouse. He ran after it, followed it up the side of a hill, but lost the mouse as it went under an old dead tree and into its roots.

The sun was setting, and he heard a deep crashing noise far away. His belly growled. *Maybe it's time to eat.* Kato looked up for Mama or Tori...but he was all alone. The deep rumble of thunder rolled through the forest. Kato wondered, *What was that?*

Sister

As it got dark, Kato walked up and down grassy hills, and then once again down along the stream. He didn't see anyone. But he could smell mice and sometimes heard squeaks coming from the bushes. His belly growled. The further he walked along, the darker it became, and the more his belly ached.

The forest was totally dark when the sky flashed bright with lightning. A loud thunderclap hurt Kato's ears. He froze in his tracks, eyes adjusting to the light. He felt a cold wind on his fur. Heavy raindrops fell from the sky through the trees. More bright flashes of lightning and louder thunder came as the wind howled. It was like the stream had been swept up into the sky and then down directly onto Kato. There was a sharp crack and then a loud thud as a branch crashed to the ground a few feet away.

Kato dug his claws into the dirt and ran. He ran and ran and ran until he found a dry spot near the trunk of a very tall tree. His little heart raced, and he could see small puffs of his breath when lightning lit up the sky. Kato shivered from the cold. His fur was wet and stuck to his skin.

Then, a long flash of lightning and a loud sound of thunder exploded right over the top of the tree above him. Frightened, Kato ran wildly into the dark, sliding on some old leaves right into some sharp thorns. He continued to slide, his wet fur showing red in a few places as Kato fell sideways into a dark hole.

****

A rough tongue licked Kato's fur and woke him up. *Where am I?* It was dark, and he could barely see two brown eyes set in a furry, grayish-brown face with a twitching tan nose. Long brown whiskers moved up and down as the rabbit continued to wash Kato." Are you okay?" asked the rabbit.

Kato was surprised he could understand the long-eared animal. The washing felt good. Kato could tell the rabbit meant no harm. He remembered seeing Mrs. Taylor chasing these animals in her garden because they ate her flowers.

"Where am I?"

"You're in my home, and you're most welcome to stay here out of the rain," said the rabbit." All of my babies have grown, and I live here all by myself."

"Have you seen my sister?" Kato asked while he rolled over and stood up. It was dark and very quiet in the rabbit hole. But Kato smelled something familiar and heard other sounds in the dark." Are we alone in here?"

"Why no, there is another kitten who wandered in here a little while ago. Just before you got here."

"Another kitten? Where?"

The rabbit pointed with its' right front paw." Well right over there."

Kato and Momma rabbit walked over to a cute little white kitten with yellow eyes that looked up, opened wide, and she purred.

"Brother!" she cried.

Kato looked at the little white kitten. *Can it really be her? Yes, it is!* He cried out, "Sister!"

Sister ran to him, sniffed him, and then rubbed her cute little pink nose on his neck. Kato squinted his eyes, sniffed Sister, and rubbed his head against hers. Sister began to lick Kato between his ears. He purred. She curled up with her brother. They both fell sound asleep purring, their front paws, hind legs, and tails intertwined.

A Feathered Friend

When they woke up, Sister told Kato how she ended up in the rabbit hole, "I was chasing mice in Mrs. Taylor's garden and wandered off too far. I couldn't find my way home. I must have walked for more than a day. I was hungry, and my belly ached. I'd only eaten a few bugs. Later I fell down the rabbit hole."

Sister stood up and stretched, arching her back. Then she sat down. Kato licked her ears, after which he told her how he'd ended up in a pale green house with a little girl named Tori.

Kato looked at Momma Rabbit and said to her, "We've got to find our way home. Can you help us?"

Momma Rabbit walked over to the kittens." I heard from a friend there's a pale green house a long walk away. I don't know exactly where. All I know is that you must cross the stream to get there."

Kato opened his eyes wide." I'll bet it's the house where Tori lives. Her mama makes delicious food." He told Sister about Tori's brothers and dad, the strange Siamese cats that didn't talk to him and about the four big dogs who played tug-of-war in the backyard.

Sister shook." I saw the stream when I was lost, but I'm afraid of the water."

Kato replied, "It's not that scary, I saw it too."

Momma Rabbit said, "The rain stopped, and the sun is now up. Why don't you two go outside and go down the hill toward the water. I'm sure it will lead you back home, and you can find something to eat."

Sister told Kato, "I'm really hungry, Brother."

Kato thought about how his own stomach rumbled. He said, "I know Sister. We'll find something in the forest. I chased some mice yesterday. With two of us, it will be easy to catch them, like we used to do at Mrs. Taylor's house."

Kato and his sister thanked Momma Rabbit and left the hole. Momma Rabbit waved goodbye and wiggled her ears as the two kittens set out, tails held high, to find the house with Tori, her family, the Siamese cats, and the dogs.

****

They heard sounds of water nearby and headed down the hill towards the noise. When they got there, Kato saw the stream was flowing much stronger now than before the storm. It sounded like it was in a hurry. It overflowed the sides of the bank. Kato and Sister walked up and down along the stream, but could not find a place to cross.

All of a sudden, a dark shadow covered the kittens. They felt a gust of wind as a strange bird flapped its wings while flying over them. The kittens watched in awe as the odd brown bird landed on a dead log.

The bird tucked his speckled wings into the sides of his body and turned around to look directly at the kittens. He had large golden eyes. Long tufts of dark feathers grew right from above his eyes, out to the side. They looked like ears. Opening his black beak, he said, "So how are you two doing this fine sunny day?"

Crossing the Stream

Kato and Sister were surprised to see such a strange looking bird standing so close to them. Sister huddled next to Kato and shivered. Kato stretched his body to its full height and bushed his tail until it looked like a bottle cleaner. Kato's ears bent back, he squeezed his eyes into narrow slits, and hissed." Hahhhhhhhh," he warned the bird who was much bigger than he was.

"Now don't be scared, little kittens," said the bird, "I mean you no harm. My mother told me to go out and fly through the woodland, to see if any forest creatures needed help after the storm last night."

Taking in a deep breath, Kato thought, *I wonder if I can trust this animal.* Then he asked, "What kind of animal are you?"

The bird puffed out his chest and said, "I'm an owl. I live with my mother in that green tree over there." He pointed with one of his wings to a very tall tree.

Kato said to the owl, "We want to cross the stream and find the pale green house, where Tori lives with her family, the Siamese cats, and the dogs. Could you help us get across the stream?"

The owl blinked his eyes and answered, "I'll fly above the water to see where you can cross." After lowering his head, he leaped into the sky. The kittens ducked as he flew over their heads with wings flapping. They watched the owl fly up and up and up until they could barely see him.

After a while, he came back and dove straight down towards them through the trees. They ducked again as the owl swooped over their heads and landed back on the old dead log. The owl said to them, "You need to walk along the stream the same way the water is flowing. After the bend, a tree has fallen across the stream, and that's where you can cross. Then follow the path on the other side, and you will find the pale green house."

Thanking the owl, Kato and Sister began walking downstream, heading for the fallen tree. The owl called out "ho-ho-hoo-hoo-hoo," and he leaped back into the air and disappeared from sight.

＊＊＊＊

Kato and his sister looked at the fallen tree lying across the stream. The water roared quickly underneath it. Swirls of white foam formed where branches and green leaves had fallen into the stream.

Sister said, "I'm afraid of the water, it moves so fast."

She's right, the water is moving very fast. But he took in a deep breath and said, "It'll be okay Sister. I'll walk across the stream first to show you it's safe."

Kato climbed over the roots of the tree to where the tree trunk broke in the storm. He jumped down onto the rough bark on the fallen tree and started to walk across the stream. The water rushed underneath him, making loud noises. His paws slid, and he almost lost his balance.

When Kato reached the middle of the stream, spray from the water hit his face and wet the tree trunk. He stepped onto a damp part of the tree, where there was no bark. His front paws slid out from under him. Kato rolled onto his side and flipped with a loud *kerplunk* into the raging cold water.

Rescue

Kato's neck stretched out from the water. He gulped for air as he floated down the rapidly moving stream. His back feet kicked in the water, trying to reach the bottom. But, he could not feel the bottom, and he could not keep his head above water. With eyes closed, he tried to hold his breath. But the water was freezing cold, and he took in a deep breath of... water.

Kato felt his body tighten, as strong, sharp toes gripped him from above and lifted him into the sky. He inhaled a lot of air, coughed, and spit out water. Kato opened his eyes and looked up at the flecked feathers of the owl. The owl held Kato as lightly as he could in his toes, so as not to hurt him with his claws. Kato looked down at the river as he was flown through the trees.

They landed in a clearing on the far side of the gully. The owl released Kato from his grip and asked him if he was OK. Kato said he was fine and the owl flew away without a sound. Kato looked to see where the owl went but collapsed shivering on the ground. His eyes closed, and everything went dark and quiet.

****

Kato felt another rough tongue licking his fur and quickly woke up. All he could see were two pale eyes in a furry white face with a twitching pink nose. Long white whiskers moved up and down as Sister washed her brother.

"Are you okay?" asked Sister.

Kato thought, *No, not really.* He said, "Sister, I'm cold, wet, and tired. How did you get here?"

"The owl came to the tree across the stream and found me. He told me about how he took you in his toes and carried you to a safe place. He asked me if I'd also like to get across the stream with his help and I told him it was okay. So, he brought me here to be with you."

Nodding his head, and thinking they were both very lucky, Kato fell asleep as Sister continued to wash him. When she was done, Sister snuggled next to him under the tree. They both were asleep as the sun set.

Mr. Coyote

The rising sun sent rays of warm golden sunlight through the trees. Kato and Sister woke up as bushes moved near them. A smiling grayish-brown head poked through the hedge and stared right at the kittens, sniffing them with a long black nose.

It looked like a large dog but was too thin to be any dog they had ever seen before. Kato immediately hissed "Hahhhhhhhh," and slowly got up on all fours. He arched his back and moved between the animal and his sister. Kato's tail puffed out, and his ears went down as he showed his claws.

"Now hold on little ones," said the animal." I'm stuck here, and I need help getting free."

Kato walked over to the animal and saw he had become all tangled up in some rope and string someone had strung between two trees. The rope had broken, and somehow the animal was all twisted up like a mummy.

Kato wondered why someone had put rope and string between trees in the woods. He figured it must be something Tori or her brothers might have done. He asked the animal, "So who or what are you?"

The animal grinned, showing all of his teeth, and said, "I'm a young Coyote all on my own. I got separated from my family and have been wandering around this area for a while. My friend, the owl, asked me if I would come over here to help you find your home." Then he looked at a tangle of ropes and string that covered his legs, arms, and body." But then I got tangled up." Coyote then looked at the kittens and showed his long and sharp teeth.

Kato wondered if he could trust this Coyote. He asked, "So how do we know you won't hurt us if we help you get free?"

Coyote looked puzzled, frowned, and after thinking for a while said, "If you free me, I'll take you to a house I know where you can get some food. I promise not to eat you." With that, Coyote held up his right paw.

Kato asked, "What house is that?"

Coyote said, "I live near a house with a fence and some yipping dogs that wander around the yard pulling on a rope playing tug-of-war. Can you believe how silly that is? And besides, those dogs don't really know how to yip. Let me show you how to yip. Yip-yip-yip-yip-yip," he barked into the sky.

Kato blinked his eyes and told his sister, "The house with the dogs sounds just like the house where Tori and her family live." He told Coyote, "I got lost from the humans who live in that house. Later I found Momma Rabbit and my sister. Then I nearly drowned in the stream until the owl saved me."

Coyote listened, cocked his head and after freeing one hind leg, he scratched his head. He said, "You're very lucky to have the owl for a friend. I've been inside the yard of that house at night and helped myself to a few chickens in back." Coyote grinned again and licked his lips.

Kato and his sister came over to Coyote and worked pulling the ropes and strings that had him tangled. They had to work for a very long time until finally, Coyote pulled himself free.

Smiling, Coyote said, "Come follow me. I'll take you to Tori's house." They all walked through the trees.

Tori's House

About the time the sun was high in the sky, the kittens' legs got very tired. Coyote looked back at them, broke into a grin, and then quickly ducked into a hole along the side of a hill. The kittens looked at each other a bit scared. *Is it safe to go into this hole?* Kato wondered. Then he and Sister followed Coyote down under the earth.

"You can rest in here," Coyote said.

Coyote's den smelled musty. It had lots of cobwebs, some small white bones, and some yellow colored bird feet scattered about. Coyote grinned and said," Don't pay any attention to my messy home, I'm going to clean it up as soon as the weather gets warmer." Kato thought the den was the messiest place he had ever seen. *Maybe we could help him clean it.*

Kato looked around and realized although the den was messy, it was, in fact, a home. *We shouldn't be so quick to judge strangers. I think we can trust Coyote even if he looks mean and lives in a mess.* Kato asked Coyote if he would wake them up after they took a nap. The kittens curled up together in a corner and purred themselves to sleep. Coyote grinned, padded over to the far corner and lay down to take a nap.

****

Later, a cold and wet nose pushed against them, "Time to get up my friends," said Coyote." You need to get through the fence and up to the house when the dogs are being fed. They won't chase you while they're eating."

Kato and his sister stretched their legs, yawned, rolled over, and then got up. Both arched their backs and extended their front legs as far as they could reach. Kato thought, *my stomach aches.* Kato told Sister to stay there and rest, while he followed Coyote to Tori's house." I'll make sure it is safe and come back with food."

Coyote and Kato followed a short path. Soon they came to a chain link fence. While smiling broadly, Coyote showed Kato where he had covered up a tunnel under the fence with some branches and leaves. Uncovering the hole, they both crawled on their bellies, under the fence, and slipped quietly into the yard.

They could hear music and smell smoke. In the distance, dogs barked. Coyote and Kato got up and followed the sounds until they saw the big pale green house. The music sounded cheerful, and the house had many bright lights outside. Smoke came from the chimney. They waited, looking at the house, and Kato's stomach grumbled. Kato thought about the wonderful food he had eaten the day he jumped from the Jeep.

****

Soon the lights in the house were turned out, and the music stopped." The dogs must be inside," said Coyote. Kato thought, *I sure hope so.* The two slowly crept up to the house, low to the ground with their tails flat down. Kato spotted the red box that Mama called a Jeep, and whispered to Coyote, "See that? That's what they drove me in when I escaped."

Coyote whispered back he often saw the red box with wheels leave the house.

"Sometimes the people take the dogs with them, and that's when I sneak into the yard to get some funny looking chickens with feathers on their cheeks. They lay blue eggs that are really delicious."

The two continued slowly inching their way up onto the front porch, staying very close to the floor and keeping their tails down. After reaching the side of the house, they rose up on their hind legs to look in through a low window.

Suddenly four dogs looked at them from indoors through the window." Ruff, ruff, ruff, ruff, ruff." Lights came on inside the house and Kato, and Coyote saw Tori's dad run to the front door carrying something long, narrow, and dark. Coyote jumped up and yelled, "Let's get out of here."

What Kind of Welcome is This?

Scared, they both ran wildly into the dark. A door opened, and they saw a bright flash of light followed by a tremendous exploding bang. Coyote let out a loud yelp, leaped into the air and disappeared into the night.

The air had a strange smell that Kato did not recognize. His little legs carried him as fast as they could. He ran down the steps, turned left towards the red Jeep, and dove underneath skidding to a stop with his face against a tire. Kato's heart pounded in his chest.

Kato heard no more loud explosions, but Tori's dad yelled something he could not understand. Kato climbed up on top of the front wheel into a dark part of the Jeep. It felt warm. His rust-colored nose wrinkled and he almost sneezed. While crawling amongst thin wires, pipes, and odd shapes, he finally found a spot that was not too bumpy. With paws tucked under his chest, he lay down and wrapped his tail alongside his body.

After a while, Kato's heart slowed down. He took in a deep breath and sighed. Inside the Jeep, it was warm and dark. *How am I going to get into the house to Tori*? In the distance, he heard a howl and knew right away his friend,

Coyote, was okay. The dogs stopped barking. The porch lights were turned out. All was dark and silent now. He was exhausted. Kato's eyes closed.

****

The Jeep's engine cooled as the night wore on. Kato began to shiver. *Was it safe to leave here? Is Tori's family angry at me or Coyote?* He missed his sister and wondered how she was. Kato listened for a while but heard nothing. He slowly crept down through the wires and pipes. Then he stopped, wrinkled his nose and sneezed. Hearing nothing, Kato jumped down onto the ground.

It was cold and dark outside, but Kato could see the steps going up to the porch. He crept up the steps and over to the window to look in. No dogs or people were in sight. Kato again thought about the delicious food Mama prepared the day he got lost. *How long ago was that? If only they knew I'm here by myself and I'm hungry.*

Kato meowed softly. Nothing moved, and no sounds were heard. He stretched up on his hind legs, his tail straight up, and looked inside as far as he could see. He meowed louder. Again nothing. Kato shivered. He went to his left, looked into a different window and cried out the third time. Nothing. Kato could smell smoke from the chimney as he moved to another window further to the left on the porch. Again, he looked inside and meowed. Nothing. His belly ached. He moved to the windows at the back of the house. Kato meowed and meowed and meowed. But no one came, and he shivered so hard his legs could hardly hold him up.

Home at Last

Some clucking noises came from the dark in the woods in back of the house. Walking through the trees up a small hill, Kato found a fence in front of a small blue building. Suddenly a large white bird ran directly towards him, on the other side of the fence. The bird made low clucking noises, as it moved its head from side to side alongside the fence, and dug into the ground with its feet. Kato jumped back from the fence and realized he was safe. The bird followed him saying "Buc, buc, buc, buc." Kato opened his eyes to look around and kept walking along the fence. *Glad that fence is between that large bird and me.*

After a short while, he noticed a larger yellow building outside the fence and walked towards it. He listened and sniffed the air near a white door, but there was no sound inside. Kato stepped through the door. The building was empty, except for a small bowl of water and something crunchy that tasted good.

He ate every scrap of food and drank all the water. When he was full, he looked around and saw a bed of straw on a shelf. So he climbed up to it and curled into a ball. Then he put his front paws over his eyes and fell soundly asleep.

****

Kato woke up to the loud crowing of "cock-a-doodle-do." He opened his eyes and looked around.

My-oh-my, what a strange way to wake up, he thought as he squeezed his eyes shut and yawned as wide as he could. Shaking his head, Kato climbed out of the straw bed and onto the platform. Sniffing the air, he walked out through the white door.

A number of large birds were cackling on the other side of the fence. The big white bird saw him again and rushed towards him while making loud noises. Kato thought, *I don't have to be afraid*. He walked away, tail held high, through the trees towards the pale green house.

Smoke oozed from the chimney, and he again sneezed. The silence was shattered by a loud "Ruff, ruff, ruff, ruff, ruff," as four dogs dashed towards him. Kato's eyes widened, and his mouth opened. He dug his claws into the dirt, ran as fast as he could away from the sound of the dogs, and up into a tree. Kato's heart pounded. The dogs jumped up the side of the tree and tried to reach him." Ruff, ruff, ruff, ruff, ruff."

Tori, her brothers, Mama and Dada, all came rushing out from the back of the pale green house. Dada asked, "Hey guys, what's all this noise?" Then they all saw what the noise was about.

Up in the tree, just above where the dogs could jump, huddled a small kitten with gray and black markings and paws that looked like they had been dipped in a can of white paint. The kitten had the most beautiful pale green-colored eyes and the cutest little rust-colored nose. He had long hair growing out of his ears. Tori and her brothers all pointed and screamed, "Its Kato! It's Kato!"

Kato was finally home.

A Family Once Again

Mama cooked some food for Kato, but all he wanted was to go and get his sister. He meowed and ran to the door. He stretched himself up along the door with both of his front legs and cried, "Meow, meow, meow, meow!"

Mama said, "What is it Kato, what do you want?"

"Meow, meow, meow, meow!" He circled while jumping up on his hind legs with his tail held high.

Tori's dad said, "What do you want little boy?"

"Meow, meow, meow, meow!" Kato again reached up against the door. *Don't they understand we need to go get Sister?*

Tori asked, "What does he want Dada?"

Mama said, "Maybe we should let him out to see what he wants?"

When they opened the side door, Kato rushed by the red Jeep and stopped. The dogs were barking again, but Tori's dad told Mama to put them on a rope. Kato looked around, sniffed the air, and then started walking towards the fence. He kept going until he saw where he and Coyote entered the yard last night.

As Dada and Kato reached the hole under the fence, Kato went through it. Tori's dad went over the fence and followed Kato along the path. Mama took Tori and the boys down to the gate.

Kato walked up to the hole in the side of the hill, where Coyote lived. He meowed and meowed. Tori's dad opened his eyes and his mouth in great surprise when he saw a skinny little white kitten with yellow eyes and a cute pink nose peek out of the hole. The kitten ran over to Kato and purred. The two kittens rubbed their heads, sniffed each other, and washed each other's ears. At long last, they would both be going home to Tori's house.

Mama and the children came through the trees. They also opened their eyes and mouths, when they saw not just Kato, but also his sister kitten! As Tori's mama and dad carried off the two kittens, the children jumped up and down and squealed as they ran in circles around their parents. *Wait till Sister tastes the good food that Mama makes.*

Coyote's nose stuck out of a bush with his teeth showing as his mouth broadened into a grin. Kato saw him, squinted his eyes slowly, and meowed a thank you for leading him and his sister back to Tori's house. Coyote let out a loud yip-yip-yip-yip-yip.

The owl sat in a tree outside the yard. He was with some crows who cackled. The owl looked at the house and said ho-ho-hoo-hoo-hoo. Kato meowed "thank you" to the owl for saving him and his sister.

Out on the road, Momma Rabbit hopped and waved. Kato meowed "thank you" for helping them find Tori's house.

****

Mama cooked up a wonderful meal and fed it to Kato and his sister. The kittens drank cream and washed faces with their paws after their soft bellies were full. Tori picked up the little white kitten and said, "You're so cute, I think I'll call you Missy." She carried Missy up the circular stairs and began to dress her up in doll's clothes, just like Tori always wanted.

Kato walked around the house with his tail held high. He was so proud of himself. He had survived in the wilderness; crossed dangerous streams, found his little sister kitten, and brought her safely to Tori's house. He had met some strange new animals and made new friends: Mother Rabbit, Wise Owl, and Sly Coyote. He might be a little kitten, but he held his chest out and felt like a big cat.

Just then, Tori's brothers came into the living room. They rolled a small ball of string towards Kato. He batted it back and the end unraveled. *Is this string the same that Coyote had been tangled in?*

The two Siamese cats stared at Kato and snarled. Kato looked directly at them. *I'm not afraid of these cats.* With that he raised his tail high and turned away from them, his hips swaying from side to side as he walked.

Kato looked at the boys and started to chase the ball of string. He thought, *I belong to the boys now.*

The rest of the family joined in the fun. Tori brought Missy down from her room, dressed in a pink tutu. *Sure glad she's dressed up and not me.* He turned back to bat the ball of string. Kato and Missy were home, together again, and safe.

Miss Kitty's French Toast
(The *Further Tails* of Miss Kitty)
Carol Hanson

Miss Kitty and her clowder mates; Glenda, Bo, and Delbert were planning a surprise. They had been living with Layla and Audrey for a year now and wanted to do something nice for them. For instance; a theme party.

Miss Kitty, in particular, had become interested in looking at different places on the globe. The other cats thought of it as a colorful spin toy, but Miss Kitty knew it had a lot to say, even with very tiny words. She had been enjoying a channel on TV that visited different places in the world. Miss Kitty would look at the globe to see if she could find them.

Miss Kitty's siblings had become interested in the computer that Layla bought, once they found out it came with a *mouse*. They thought this would be an easy way to snag some unsuspecting mice. Alas, they didn't understand that the mouse with the computer was not a rodent.

Miss Kitty wanted to celebrate Audrey's birthday. She had heard Layla discussing it with her. Audrey was going to be ten on July 14, and this meant that she would be entering the world of double digits. This on its own was a reason to celebrate.

Miss Kitty had watched a TV show on France and learned that their noisy celebration day was on July 14 and was called Bastille Day. It was similar to the noisy celebration day humans celebrated, which all in all was about independence. The fireworks on TV were a whole lot quieter than the ones done outside. The Paris fireworks had this cool tower that was famous, and it looked like the fireworks were coming out of the tower.

When the brothers heard Miss Kitty mention Bastille their ears perked up. "Bass," mewed Delbert. "Sounds like a bluish green fish to me," piped in Bo. Miss Kitty and Glenda were both about to roll their eyes but knew that before this party got going, they would probably be rolling their eyes multiple times.

Miss Kitty wanted to make French foods for Audrey's party. She wasn't sure how much help her siblings would be, but everyone had to come up with a French food. Glenda said: "I got dibs on French Fries." Miss Kitty called out "French Toast." Bo and Delbert were for once at a loss for words. Delbert optioned for Belgian waffles, which were quickly eliminated from the French menu. Bo yelled out "French Dressing" before his brother took it as his food. Delbert tried again. "How about French Twist?" Miss Kitty kindly told him that a French twist was a hairdo.

Delbert hemmed and hawed for a moment or two, then suddenly shouted "Three French hens!" Delbert had remembered a song that Audrey sang when she and Layla were putting things on a tree inside the house during the cats' first cold weather stay in a warm house. He had later learned that the tree in the house was called a Christmas tree. Delbert had seen one outside that was similar but found out it was a jack pine tree. Their tree was a spruce he learned, and on no uncertain terms were the cats allowed to think of it as a toy. Paws off!

Miss Kitty agreed that they must have a protein with the dinner. Delbert was about to ask what was a protein and then thought better of it since everyone agreed that three French hens would work very well. He hoped Audrey wasn't going to sing that repetitive Christmas song again, but it was going to be her special day.

So now they had a menu. The cats told Layla about their idea. Layla suggested a salad to put *under* the French dressing. The cats didn't care for salad, but they knew Audrey liked it. Layla also thought she would try her hand at French Onion soup. She thought the cats had come up with a great idea. She just didn't know how they were going to be able to pull off a surprise.

Audrey had asked to spend the night at her friend's house. Everyone thought this would be a great chance to make some of the foods in advance. Each of the cats thought that whatever they were going to make would be the highlight of the meal. Layla decided to make a chart to let everyone know when it would be their turn to work in the kitchen.

The cats all waited patiently; well, some more than others, to create their concoction. Layla knew this would be a hands-on experience for everyone. She just didn't know that they would all be covered in flour and other ingredients along the way. Thank goodness, they had time to recover and clean up. Layla knew that German Chocolate Cake and German Chocolate Ice Cream were Audrey's favorite desserts. She just didn't know how she was going to break this to the cats that she was tweaking the French menu. She decided to call them: Dessert One and Dessert Two!

Layla had arranged for Audrey to come home around noon. She couldn't believe that they had actually succeeded in getting everything done. *Voila!* Red, white, and blue balloons were hung, as Miss Kitty reminded them that France's flag had the same colors as the American flag. Glenda was so proud of her sister. She always had the best ideas.

When Audrey walked in the house, she was flanked by the cats. Layla greeted her with a big birthday hug. They sat down to their French feast, and Miss Kitty had everyone clink their glasses, so she could make a toast; a French toast that is. After the toast, the other cats chimed in *Viva la Audrey!* So many good things had happened since these cats came into their lives. Audrey couldn't remember a happier day.

Morning After Ballet
Sarah Milne Das

The staircase was not quite as bad as the rest of the house, but it was bad, nevertheless. Cigarette stubs floated in the dregs of some cheap and nasty red; beer cans were littered up the steps in varied states of flattenedness, and a semi-crushed watermelon was lodged precariously between two of the upright rails supporting the sticky banister.

Bella and Mischa sat on the top step surveying the wreckage. Bella, somewhat of a veteran, betrayed just a touch of distaste with the slight scrunch of her elegant nose. She had, some forty minutes ago, nudged open an Asda magazine to a spread on tropical fruit deals, set this down on the floor, and deliberately settled herself on top of it so as to avoid the damp carpet. Mischa, meanwhile, as the house's newest resident, could barely contain her excitement at this new and decadent experience, at being party to such extreme post-bacchanalic squalor. Cocking her head to one side and listening intently for any sound behind them, she nudged Bella's shoulder with hers: "It doesn't sound like he's getting up."

Bella gave a ladylike yawn as she leant back in a leisurely stretch." No," she drawled." He has a *girl* in there."

"A *girl*! One of *our* girls?" Mischa's eyes opened wide, and she continued in a breathless rush, "I saw Lucy being sick in the umbrella stand earlier, and then she went to lie down in the garden. Right on the grass, I saw her. She said..." and Mischa crumpled her face in concentration, "...the dew would 'wake her up and serve her right, and she wasn't ever doing it again'..."

"She *always* says that after a *party*," scoffed Bella." No, it's not one of *our* girls in there. It's one of their friends, one of that lot that were giggling and screeching away last night. He *always* has a girl there after a *party*, and Lucy and Hannah are always *livid* when they find out, because 'how are they going to explain to their friends that he's a total utter wanker, and he promised he wouldn't this time, not if he was going to sweet talk some poor gullible thing into bed then ignore all her texts afterwards, and it's embarrassing to have to warn every female with a pulse that you live with a *complete. lech.*'"

"Well then," said Mischa, eager to show off some worldly wisdom, "he's in for it now, isn't he? Someone *is* going to be cross when they find out he's done it *again*." She hesitated before trying out a more woman of the world-esque tone: "Rather a *bore*."

"As a matter of fact, someone is *already* cross, Mischa, because *I* am cross." Bella drew herself up self-importantly." He dropped his horrid beer on my bed last night, and now it's damp and smells like the canal. It's *foul*. I had to go and sleep with Hannah, who-" she shuddered, "*cuddled* me then cried on me then had to run to the loo."

"Oh," said Mischa in a small voice.

"*Oh*," said Bella, in a superior one.

They sat, again, in companionable silence.

Sometime later, the nearby bedroom door creaked open, and a pair of naked legs walked out, attached, as Bella has foretold, to one of last night's giggling girls. She was wrapped in a rather threadbare towel, and almost tripped over Mischa before stopping short in surprise.

"The *kitties*!" she squealed, "Oh my goodness! Pete, do your lovely cats always wait here to say good morning?"

A grunt and Pete called grumpily back." Not mine. Wasn't my idea to get bloody cats. That slinky one's a right bitch as well. She doesn't like me, I know it."

The girl ignored him as she fussed over them both, Mischa cavorting with kittenish excitement, and Bella preening, allowing herself to be stroked, and butting her head gently at the girl in an extremely uncharacteristic show of affection.

"Oh, aren't you two *beautiful*? Who's a gorgeous cat, who's a gorgeous cat?" After an appropriate period of homage, the girl reluctantly pulled away from them and looked around absently." Oh, I must leave you two alone now, I was going to jump in the shower while it's free..." Directing a final beaming smile at them, she adjusted the towel around herself and crossed the landing to the bathroom, just as Hannah emerged, disheveled, from her bedroom, took in the situation at a glance, and groaned.

Several things then happened at once. The sound of the shower running started up. Bella took several unexpected leaps across the furniture to the nearby high shelf that was her habitual hiding place, then leapt back down again via Hannah's shoulder. Poor hungover Hannah was so startled by this that she jumped out her skin with a stifled scream, and the chaos outside his bedroom moved Pete to drag himself up and stomp downstairs, all the while muttering and swearing to himself about hysterical females and nuisance felines.

In the relative calm that followed Pete's departure, Hannah sighed with relief and rubbed her eyes wearily, then something caught her eye, and she stooped down over the cats, puzzled." Bella, what's that you're playing with? Where did you get that bottle, it had better not be something expensive..."

Mischa, who had been happily distracted by the humans' drama, now also looked over at Bella, who was indeed batting a small bottle between her two front paws, looking the picture of inscrutable innocence. Hannah picked up the bottle to a hiss of displeasure, and frowned." Lotion, men's, oh *Bella*. Why do you always take *Pete's* things when you're making mischief? It's like you *know* it annoys him."

She tossed the bottle into Pete's room, where it landed softly on the bed, then looked at the cats with exasperated fondness." Come on then, trouble and trouble, let's see about some breakfast, shall we?"

As she made for the stairs with Mischa at her heels, Bella determinedly turned her back and stalked in the opposite direction, tail swishing with offence." Oh, suit yourself then," called Hannah over her shoulder, "but don't come meowing to me when you realise you're hungry!"

There was, however, a little more to this apparent fit of pique than either Hannah or Mischa realised. Within seconds of them disappearing out of sight, Bella had turned tail again and padded surreptitiously into Pete's room.

When he returned moments later and saw the lotion spilled over the bedclothes and Bella lounging across the pillow contentedly, a bellow of frustration burst out of him." For the love of -" he picked her up roughly and dropped her to the floor before grabbing a box of Kleenex and beginning to mop up the mess.

As Bella scurried out of the room he followed her and started to call downstairs, "Hannah, that *bloody* cat is...what the hell is it doing now!"

Bella was attacking the trapped watermelon, launching herself at it repeatedly with claws out, spraying liquid and pulp everywhere. Pete yanked the watermelon out from the rails and clutched it under one arm, grabbing a yowling Bella in the other and stamping back up the stairs.

She broke free as he reached the landing and pelted to his room. Pete, with a curse, bent to pick up the magazine from the top of the stairs and rolled it up to give Bella a frustrated slap. She ran through his legs in a figure of eight and streaked away as he tumbled to the floor. Pete flung away the magazine and dropped the watermelon as he flailingly tried to save himself, but gravity was still gravity, and he landed heavily with a moist squelch.

It was at this moment that the girl returned, humming happily to herself. She seemed not to have heard any of the commotion, but when she reached Pete's doorway, she stopped dead.

On his bed lay an open bottle of lotion and a box of Kleenex, next to the Asda magazine which had fallen open at the page with the tropical fruit. Pete himself was struggling up from the floor, where he'd landed crotch-first in the soggy watermelon.

There was a silence as the girl looked at Pete, at the bed, and back at Pete, then she snatched up her clothes and started angrily to get dressed." Jesus, Pete, I was just in the shower, weren't you worried I was going to walk in on you... you..."

The realization had gradually dawned on Pete that he was centre-stage in a tableau with less than savoury implications." It's not what it looks like! I wasn't... That bloody *cat*!"

"What the hell are you talking about? No, wait, I don't care. I should have listened to Hannah, you are...I don't even know what you are! I'm going home!" And she stormed out, slamming the door noisily behind her.

Downstairs, Hannah winced at the bang, then raised her eyebrows in amusement." Well, that didn't take long!" she remarked to the cats as she set down two bowls before them.

Bella smirked and started on breakfast.

Oswald, The Magnificent Protector of Potted Plants
Sarah M. Lewis

I walk into the house and find pots of plants in my sunny spot. Plants don't belong inside. Plants belong outside. Plants are for a cat to stalk through, climb on, or hide behind, an aid for pouncing on birds, mice, moles, and snakes. Hunting is not so good now when it's cold outside. Green plants go brown, and their leaves are gone.

Plants are no use in the house. A-ha! I get it. This is Ashley's mom's revenge for my breaking all the mugs on her counter.

I had to do it. No self-respecting cat like me would put up with Ashley bringing a strange boy onto my territory. Ashley didn't bring him over and let me check him out. He made no attempt to show submission to me. They sat there, papers covering the kitchen table, paying no attention to me.

"Al-ge-bra. Al-ge-bra." They said instead of, "Thank you, Oswald, for keeping an eye on us."

I climbed up on the counter and pushed over the first mug as fair warning.

Crash.

Nobody ignores Oswald. I am the cat.

"Oswald! Crazy Cat!"

I'm not crazy. I know what I'm doing. Pay me my respect or the next mug goes down.

Crash.

"Oswald! Stop it right now!"

A half-grown girl thinks she can give an order to this cat? I push another one over.

Crash.

"Wait till Mom sees this."

Yes. Then, Mom will know her Ashley's manners need correcting.

Ashley's mom came home. What does she do? Does she use her whopping-paw voice on Ashley when she sees the broken mug? No. She calls me "Bad Cat."

I didn't accidentally knock things over like a kitten having a hissy fit. I deliberately destroyed her mugs one by one, indicating my righteous anger at Ashley's disrespect.

I was so shocked I laid my ears back instead of washing my paws and ignoring her.

Ashley's mom walks right past me with the watering pot and pours water on those stupid plants. She makes cooing noises to them and talks to them. "Have a drink of water, baby."

I'm worried about her. She knows plants don't talk back.

Plants don't say "meow" and "err" which mean, "Feed me. Pet me. Let me in. Let me out. Give me more room in bed. I want this side of the couch. Turn the TV down, I'm trying to sleep."

Plants won't rub her legs, marking her with their scent, letting every other animal with a nose know Oswald, a cat with claws and teeth loves and protects her.

I walk over, giving her a chance to say, "Oswald, you are the most amazing, magnificent cat of all!"

"Oswald! Don't bump the plants over. Oswald, those stems aren't play toys; don't bat them! Oswald, don't bite that leaf! Go eat your cat-food. Oswald! No! No! No!"

Ashley's mom pets those plants. She's supposed to pet me.

Ashley offers me a head rub as I duck under the kitchen table full of those papers she's laid out all over it. "Mom just wants the geraniums to make it through winter, Oswald. She'll put them outside when it gets warm."

I better hang with Ashley. I put my paws on her lap, offering to climb up and allow her to cuddle my royal catness. Ashley pushes me away. Me! Away! "Not now, Oswald. I have to pass my algebra test tomorrow."

I think I hate the word "algebra" almost as much as "No. No."

When Ashley's best friend Shameka didn't invite Ashley to her birthday party, I let Ashley cry all over me. I didn't wriggle off her lap and head out to chase a sassy Chihuahua off my turf. No, I was there for Ashley till Shameka called and the two of them made up.

When Ashley's mom was afraid the insurance wouldn't call about fixing her car, I sat in her lap purring for her to hold onto even when she held me so hard it hurt. Plants can't do that.

She will put her plants outside when it gets warm, will she? I'm a well-furred cat. I will put myself outside in the cold and let them see how well they do with those plants, but without me.

I hear Mom and Ashley calling, "Oswald. Here kitty, kitty."

I don't come. I hear them slam the door. "Stay out all night!"

Next day I come in calm and casual.

Ashley's mom says, "Don't bump into the plants, Oswald. See, I moved your food bowl out of the way."

No "Welcome home. We missed you, Oswald." I check out my food bowl. What's going on? Where's my wet food? All I've got is dry food.

"We're out of your wet food. I'll get some on the way home from work," Ashley's mom tells me.

I dump out my bowl scattering dry food over the floor.

"Oswald!"

I walk over to those plants, my ears laid back flat, and knock over the first pot, before heading out my cat door. I may need to think about finding a new home if things don't change around here. Every cat's dignity is all cats' dignity.

That evening there's wet food, and Ashley comes home happy. "I passed my algebra test."

She pats her lap. "Want a lap, Oswald?"

Well, okay. I jump up and allow her to rub my head, though her head-rubbing is not as good as her mom's.

I spend most of the cold time when days are short and nights long visiting other people who pay me for protection. They show me their appreciation.

Mrs. Johnson gives me fried chicken and says, "Oh great snake killer, keep it up."

Mr. Brown gives me tuna and says, "You. The Exterminator."

The days began to get longer and warmer. One day I come home for breakfast, and those pesky plants are outside in my yard, their pots lined up in one of my favorite outdoor snoozing spots.

I go inside for breakfast. I'm not even finished eating when the woman starts fussing.

"Oswald! Bad cat!"

"What's Oswald done now?" Ashley asks.

"He's turned over two of the geranium pots."

Two of the pots are turned over. Hey, I'm right here at my food bowl, an innocent cat! I didn't do it.

"I guess he's still jealous," Ashley says.

Of a plant! If I wanted to murder a plant, I've got the paws to dig it up by its roots. I've got the claws to shred it with. I've got the teeth to chew up pieces and spit them out.

Next day it's "Oswald, stop knocking over the geraniums, or so help me."

I go over to sniff around the area. My nose and whiskers twitch. I can smell another animal was there.

"Aaugh!"

The spray from the hose knocks me over. I race for the fence.

"Oswald, I told you to get away from those plants."

How can I find out who knocked over those plants if I get sprayed with water every time I get near them?

Three days, I've stayed far away from those plants. Ashley's mom can see I'm not the one turning them over, but she still yells at me every time she finds one turned over. I wait until she's not looking before creeping over to check the pots; my ears open for the sound of Ashley's mom inside walking to the windows.

I smell it. One of those tree-climbing, bushy-tailed rats called squirrels. I see its tracks all around the pots.

"Oswald, get away from the geraniums."

I walk away before Ashley's mom can turn the hose on me again.

Then I position myself behind a bush and wait, and wait and wait. Hunting is waiting. My ears pick up the pitter patter of squirrel feet. My whiskers quiver. I feel its wind as it scampers among the geranium pots. It stands up looking around.

I flatten myself to the ground and crawl forward on my belly, noiseless as a snake in the grass.

The squirrel stands up, its nose quivering. It begins to push on a geranium pot.

I am close, getting closer.

"Mom, it's the squirrel." I hear Ashley. She must be looking out the glass doors.

The squirrel rocks the pot back and forth.

I pounce and barely miss. If it had hit the ground before turning around, I would have had it. It races for the fence with me on its heels. It leaps to the top of the fence, back to me, switching its tail up and down and chittering. I crouch below lashing my tail.

The squirrel goes into the next yard, and I walk back to the house with my head high, whiskers spread, and my tail up. "You owe me, Oswald the magnificent, an apology."

Later, reclining among the geranium pots, I've decided that red flowers make the purrfect background to show off my magnificent catness to the world.

Pizazz
Elisabeth Ward

We found her as a kitten, maybe 5-weeks old, hiding in terror inside a burglar gate outside a Manhattan shop. It was early morning. Mothers walked young children to the numerous nearby Upper East Side schools. Dogs accompanied their families on the daily excursion, but this day was different. Everyone stopped to look inside the gate. Picture this scene from inside that burglar gate:

Street noise. Many feet, some with shiny or squeaky shoes, some with high pointy heels, some with fur and long toenails. Bald faces showed bared irregular patterns of teeth surrounded by lengths of hair or baseball caps, or furry faces with panting red tongues and huge teeth. Odd sounds such as *oooo* and *ohhhh* and squeals of *cuuute*.

The story circulated, going up the street with the children and down the street with the returning mothers telling latecomers: Three kittens either fell or were pushed from the second-story window. One of them landed softly in an open garbage can. Dawn brought the grinding rumble of a garbage truck and the burly men who emptied the lined-up containers into the truck's hold. The kitten leapt to safety. Small enough to fit easily through the end openings in the burglar gate, it tried to hide in a far corner. But these burly, can-throwing men saw her, stuck rolled-up magazines in each end to prevent escape, then rushed up the street, away from its hiding place.

Relief was brief, for they returned and began throwing things at the kitty, who was too frightened to notice these things were small and smelled good. Certainly, it could not read the bags those large hands ripped open, was not familiar with *Tender Vittles*. The big men left as the little creatures with the piping voices arrived. The kitten alternated between flight (from one side of the opening to the other and back) and fight (a barely audible *hisss* with miniature teeth and tiny paw spread to reveal claws the size of, well, those of a five-week-old kitten).

I'd spent fifteen years with a traumatized cat. Maybe I could help this one. The first thing was to leave the kitty alone. I hung up a sign: THIS CAT IS BEING TAKEN CARE OF. PLEASE IGNORE IT. She watched me, arched her back, hissed, raised a paw in threat. I gasped in (mock) horror and retreated. The last thing this kitten needed was lack of confidence in her ability to frighten away danger.

Our young daughter had been given a child-sized version of a wicker fishing creel—six-inch-long, two compartments with jointed lids below the handle, one lid opening from each end. This looked about the right size to hold the kitten on one side, my wallet and a small can or two or cat food on the other. I called our veterinarian, collected the creel, a pair of cotton gloves, our twenty-pound shaggy dog, and returned to the shop to await the owner's arrival. By this time the crowds had passed, and the kitten felt the chill that follows exertion. The early April sun had moved to a near corner of the gate. The kitten crept into it and fell asleep, back to, but not touching, the gate.

Our dog sniffed the tiny lump, then curled up in the sun on the outside corner, back to but not touching, the gate. I sat on the sidewalk next to her, speaking quietly, before poking an index finger through the bars and gently prodding behind a bony shoulder blade. First, the kitty flinched slightly. Five minutes later, as my hand moved to rub her little-fingertip size triangular ear, her body started to vibrate—not with fear but with the first rumbles of a purr.

The shop's owner arrived midmorning. She greeted the dog and me politely but quizzically, as the kitten was not visible—even after I explained the situation.

"There," I pointed to a brown lump no larger than a medium wadded-up paper napkin, "there it is."

It stood up when the shopkeeper set key to lock and slowly lifted the gate, which didn't have to go far for me to collect the kitten in one gloved palm. I slipped the glove off under the kitty as I placed both into one side of the creel, then put the other glove on top before lowering the lid. The rumbling stopped, but there was no scrabbling, no hissing or frantic wail. The creel simply tilted slightly—ever so slightly—as the kitty burrowed into the gloves.

By the time we'd walked to the vet and sat in the waiting room for a spell, the kitty was accustomed to my voice and the scent of the dog who constantly sniffed through the wicker.

"Name?" asked the vet, pen in hand, as we entered the examination room.

Hmm, the cat didn't look like a sanitation worker. The burglar gate had kept it in, not out. It had refused the Tender Vittles. What *was* the name of that shop three doors down from the corner? I pictured the street.

"Pizazz," I answered." The name is Pizazz."

Surprisingly, for a girl of the streets, Pizazz checked out all right. We made an appointment for shots when she came of age, and we walked back home with a stop at the grocery store.

"You look like you could use some liver," I said to the creel as I read cat food labels. For some reason, this statement to a child's wicker fishing creel caught surprised looks from two women turning into our aisle.

I carefully lifted the lid on Pizazz's side, and up popped her bright blue-eyed, curious face. She showed neither fear nor eagerness to escape, just proof that she was an astonishingly adorable kitten with perfect tiger stripes pointing to those eyes and, when she closed them to settle down, markings above each eye that made them appear open and watchful.

On the way home from the grocery store we stopped at that shop three doors down from the corner, where I introduced Pizazz to the owner of Pizazz.

Once home I took Pizazz to the guest room that doubled as playroom and study. I placed food and water under the bed and a Sara Lee tin of kitty litter in the corner. I put Pizazz in the litter box, then watched her walk across our soft-pile rug. She was so small she had trouble keeping her balance, so I tucked her under the bed, closed the door and left.

When our two children came home from school they were told to play elsewhere, but allowed to look under the bed—once—and then leave, for this kitty needed confidence. That's something young children understand.

By the second day, Pizazz was waiting when I opened the door to her room. By the third day, the children were allowed to play board games on the floor if they ignored the kitty. This was fine for Pizazz but not so great for Monopoly. Every time the kids left the room the kitty would bat those irresistible green houses around the board and disappear under the bed before being caught in the act.

Over the weekend when my six-foot three-inch husband stretched out atop our bed for a nap, Pizazz pussy-footed into the bedroom, climbed the bedspread and then my husband's ankle. She was so small he slept on as she walked precariously along his leg, then his torso, hopped down and circled his head, scaled a shoulder and, exhausted, fell asleep on his chest. Having thus conquered the largest creature in our home she had no further fears. Ever.

Twenty-three years later Pizazz purred herself into the next world from her lofty position as the head of our animal family, curled between our two large Weimaraners and our daughter's French bulldog. The shaggy dog who raised her taught her well: first, make a terrible noise, then go about your business. Over her years as a country cat and traveling companion Pizazz also trained two family pit bulls, a Lhasa Apso and any strange dog or cat—or fox—to *Obey the Cat.*

The shop three doors down from the NYC corner? Long gone. But, it had been the right place at the right time to provide the right name. Cats know. We just have to let them prove it.

Rescue
Dexter Morales

I saw an ad for you in the paper.
They said you had been
Left at the door.
A pound is no place
To start a life.

You were too young
To even be away from
Your mother.

Belly full of worms,
So skinny your bones were showing,
Hair all in a mess,

But –

I could tell you had some fight in you.
After a few visits to the vet
You began to blossom.

We have been together five years now,
And no one would ever guess what
Life was like for you
In the beginning.

You taught me the many
Rewards of adoption.
Since our journey began
Three more have joined
Our small pride.

Resistance Is Futile
Patricia Walkow

How did it get to this point?

My beloved inky black rescue cat, Moxie, is showing some signs of age. He takes (I force down his throat) gastrointestinal medication, and I have been experimenting with a variety of foods to determine what he likes and what his system will tolerate. The prescription diet proffered by his veterinarian was a failure. Neither he, my younger adopted cat, Maggie, or even the dog would touch it.

If a dog won't eat something, you know for sure a cat won't.

I find myself reading every word of canned cat food labels in the pet food specialty stores." Specialty" is a synonym for "expensive." These are retail establishments where a three-ounce can of wet cat food can set you back between $1.29 and $2.99 in 2017 dollars.

Many cats ago, my little felines ate twenty-five-cents-a-can tuna or chicken cat foods—nothing sophisticated. Now, cats have become gourmets. It seems they require their food to have organically-grown spinach or heirloom sweet potatoes in some sort of gourmet concoction. Do they secretly subscribe to *Epicurean Feline* or *Tomcat Gourmand* magazine? Have we cat lovers raised their expectations to unsustainable levels?

Does Moxie want tuna today? Should it be shredded, in paté, or nuggets or slices? Heavy sauce or light sauce? Gluten-free? Grain free? Organic? Sustainably harvested?

Not in the mood for tuna? How about salmon? Wild salmon? Trout? Mackerel? Sole? A mixture? Grilled, stewed, pureed, or braised? Poached?

When he prefers meat, Moxie might eat chicken or turkey, or duck, or elk, or beef, or bison, or rabbit. Do you want chicken today, my precious? Free range only, you say? Feeling vegetarian today, Mox?

He devours seafood. One week it might be wild Alaskan salmon; the following week he might sneer at it and prefer North Atlantic wild cod.

Since my two cats don't eat only wet food, I find myself in the same predicament with dry food.

Moxie is not as choosy about his dry food as he is with the canned stuff, although if I give him a dry food variety that is healthy for him, he doesn't want it just by itself. He acts out, as cats do, by trying to cover it the same way he covers you-know-what in the litter box. I resort to mixing the expensive premium dry food with the equivalent of kitty junk food, made mostly of grain and meat by-products. *Then* he'll eat it.

There are dry cat foods for indoor cats, longhaired cats, kittens, mid-life cats, senior cats, arthritic cats, cats with sensitive stomachs, lactating cats, cats with kidney issues, cats with allergies, cats with dental problems. So far, I have not found one for cats with emotional issues.

Occasionally I splurge on prosciutto, a smoked ham from Parma, Italy, for myself. Pound for pound, it is cheaper than some premium cat foods.

Then there are kitty treats. These are diminutive delicacies packaged in appealing little plastic bottles or colorful foil-lined bags. They have endearing names like Temptations®, Whisker Lickings'®, Party Mix™, Kittles™, Savory Bites® and Party Mix™.

Whether one refers to them as *hors-d'oeuvres*, appetizers or *tapas*, most cats find them scrumptious.

These treats can be soft or hard, round or square, solid, hollow or stuffed. Old boy Moxie does not care if I place them in his regular food dish, in a Tiffany crystal bowl, or on the floor. He would like me to replace his dry food with all treats, but I refuse.

Younger Maggie, however, is considerably more discerning about her treats. At three years old, she is an authentic aficionado of these tiny edible delights. She could be a member of a cat treat focus group for determining which products to bring to market.

Maggie can sniff a treat for an hour. She has a special oval plate on the kitchen counter, just for her treats. Usually, I place one morsel in it. She will look at me and then commence her elaborate olfactory examination. Convinced I have not pleased her, I will place a different kind of treat next to the first one. She stares at me, then inhales the scent of the delicacies in her plate. Sometimes I offer her a third edible delight. She will peer intently at me, then reduce her eyes to arrogant, accusatory slits, as though to say, "Do you actually expect me to eat these? You gave me the same cocktail snacks yesterday."

Disappointed with me, she will jump off the counter and leisurely swagger away, her patrician tail held high, then flicked in utter disgust. Although I know it is an act, I still feel I have failed her royal highness. Ten minutes later, when she thinks I won't notice, she will come back and devour everything in her porcelain treat dish, like the starving stray she once was.

When I was younger, I would not tolerate this nonsense from my cats.

I ran the show.

However, over the years, all the cats I have loved and sheltered have trained me to do their bidding. That's the reason two cats have six beds scattered around the house, a foodie's paradise of a pantry, padded window seats with a view to outdoors, and bird feeders within sight. The cats sleep on my bed, on my desk, on my computer's keyboard, on top of the piano, *inside* the piano, in the bathtub, on the exact paragraph of the newspaper article I am reading, on the top shelf of my closet, and on my chest. My new washing machine has a clear glass top so they can amuse themselves with the laundry. The salesman thought I was kidding when I told him I wanted the glass lid for my cats.

I reached this point of acquiescence to my cats' desires due to the excellent instruction I received from my previous cats. Moxie and Maggie are the fortunate heirs to all my training and to the fact I no longer resist the demands and expectations of the feline inhabitants of the planet.

The truth? I am vanquished. And, as they say on Star Trek, "Resistance is futile."

The Cat Got Paddled
A.J. Huffman

she said, and I immediately thought, how lazy.
Feline or not, it could have at least grabbed an oar,
helped its owner row the craft, like that famous pussycat
who went to sea in an ugly-colored boat. It's not
like a little work would kill it, and even it there was
some strange waving accident, the furry critter would still have
eight lives left.

"down the stairs by my father," she finished
her sentence, and I swallowed my previous
critique with total shame. That poor cat.
I felt awful for it, and its ass. Those wooden paddle games
are thin and cheaply made, easy for even children to break,
but I suspect repeated contact, even though fur would still hurt
like hell.   Not to mention the awkward discomfort that must
have ensued in order to get that retractable rubber
string affixed to its tail.

The Cat That Changed My Life

Susan P. Blevins

I looked in the mirror and finished tarting myself up for a night out on the town with friends, and let myself out of the big wooden front door to the apartment building where I lived. I had been living in Rome for many years by this point and had a multitude of friends, so my social calendar was always crammed with exciting dates: lots of cocktails on Via Veneto, glamorous dinners, way too many clothes, and of course, lots of sex with lots of lovers. Truth be told, this was beginning to wear on me, and my happiness felt superficial and hollow. Surely there had to be more to life than just having fun. This uneasiness had prompted me to go into Jungian psychotherapy recently, with an analyst who was a bit of a dragon! One time she had reprimanded me by saying, "If you don't follow the truth of your dreams, you can stop wasting your money and my time." Strong words, which left their mark and which I strove to heed.

But here I was, dressed up and setting out against my better judgment for a frivolous evening, while underneath lurked the distinct feeling that I should have refused the invitation, and stayed home and read worthwhile books, or engaged in some other *meaningful* activity. How was I going to justify it to my analyst?

I started walking down my street towards my parked car, telling myself this was the last time I would go out with this bunch of rowdy, hedonistic friends. I put the key in the lock of my little Fiat 500, slid into the seat, turned on the ignition, and started to maneuver myself out of the tight parking space. I had just pulled out into the deserted street, about to accelerate away for the evening, when I saw the most beautiful Siamese cat I had ever seen in my life walking down the sidewalk toward me. Well, I am cat mad, so I immediately re-parked the car and got out.

I approached the elegant seal point feline, babbling to it (I didn't know if it was male or female at this point). "So, who are you?" I gushed. "Where did you come from darling?" He made no move to escape from me, so I scooped him up in my arms whispering words of love. He started to purr immediately. Mutual adoration. I was instantly, totally, head over heels in love with this little boy.

Well, goodbye night out on the town, and hello to an evening of bliss adjusting to my new companion. I made a half-hearted attempt to find a previous owner on my short street, but he was wearing no collar and was not chipped as cats are here in the USA. I thought that it was fate that had brought him to me at such a pivotal moment in my life, so I kept him. At least I knew there was now one less abandoned cat wandering the streets of Rome. In recognition of the wisdom he had displayed in choosing *me* above all others to stroll up to, I named him Solomon. I have had cats ever since I was born and loved them all, but Solomon became without a doubt the love of my life.

I felt it was divine providence that had sent Solomon to me so serendipitously, to save me from myself! Had I emerged from the building just five minutes earlier, or five minutes later, I would have missed him, and my life would have continued its confused wanderings as before. But after he came into my life I had no further desire to go out socializing, and from then on, I trod with great devotion the path of psychoanalysis, Solomon always my comfort and companion, in fact, I considered him my psychopomp. How fortunate that I had recognized him as God's messenger, to keep me on the straight and narrow path of my soul's journey, because who knows, had he not appeared, I may have turned my back on the exacting rigors of psychoanalysis and continued my meaningless, superficial life, wondering why I was not happy, frittering away precious time.

The Cat
A. Elizabeth Herting

The cat extends himself to his full length, peeking through the window. He lets out a hearty meow, shattering the tomb-like silence of the old house. He is a funny looking little creature, a black koala bear nose nestled on a white face, like negative film exposed too long in the light. He has a patch of black on one leg, another completely white. His black and white, yin and yang markings swirl around in confused, disorganized perfection. The very epitome of what a molly gowser, short-haired, respectable alley cat should be. He prowls the perimeter of the house, drawn to it by some inexplicable instinct that makes him yowl in feline delight. Having no luck at the front window, he heads around to the back door, scratching and clawing at it in his impatience.

Anne jumps up with a start, almost dropping the crystal wine glass she had been cleaning. What is that unearthly sound? She sets the glass back down on the dining room table and sighs at the sight. Glasses, dishes, pots and pans, cups as far as her eye can see sit out on every surface, waiting to be organized. In fact, the living room is completely filled, every inch covered with clothing, Tupperware, cooking utensils, loose bits of bric-a-brac-- the contents of an entire life, unvarnished and on full display. Anne sighs and picks up the fortifying glass of wine on the counter, taking a big sip. There is no way that I can ever get through all of this, she thinks in despair. I don't even want to. The Estate Sale is tomorrow, the day of reckoning. She has put out the signs, the ads have been posted and reposted, now all she has to do is throw the doors open and sell all of her childhood memories to complete strangers. What's not to love about that?

The cat gets no response at the back door, but he is not deterred. He rounds the garage and sees a large picture window, light streaming through. He gets a running start and launches himself onto it with claws fully extended. He hits it at full speed, a loud crunch breaking through the thick window pane, before landing hard in the bushes. He slinks away to regroup, truly embarrassed in the way that only cats can be at anything less than complete gracefulness.

Anne is amazed at the folks she has met coming and going in her parents' house today. She would never have expected to find so much goodness, followed by sheer greed. More than one person wanted to give her a hug and share their stories, while another special soul offered to buy her father's coffin flag for $10. They rifled through every part of this place, looking for items even in the medicine cabinets, hall closets, drawers, kitchen cabinets, spices—nothing was off limits. It was a huge success, as far as these things go, so why do I feel like I need a shower?

Anne drags the last few bags down to the end of the driveway. This is it, the last of it, going off to Goodwill. It is finally over. A flash of something white catches her eye and speeds off into the bushes. What was that, a rabbit? The bush emits a loud meow, as if in answer to her unspoken question. Anne immediately feels a pang of guilt. Mom had three cats, and I just had to find a home for them. There was no way I could take them all and the older two were a package deal, having been together their entire lives. A nice young couple had come over in response to her animal rescue posting and taken the pair of old Maine Coon Cats off to their new, and hopefully happy, home. God, getting them packed up and into the car was heartbreaking. The cats had lived in that house for over 10 years. They were everything to Mom, filling her life in the years after Dad died. Anne makes a quick decision and heads back into the house, searching for her mother's supply of dried cat food.

The cat, having just finished his second midmorning nap, takes one last, luxurious stretch and ventures out of the bush in search of food. He can smell something in the air. He is an expert in these things, following the smell eagerly around to the front porch of the house. Seeing the source of his good fortune, he rushes forward and falls upon his prize, crunching and gulping in pure feline ecstasy.

Anne tries to stifle a giggle as she watches the cat gorging on the small bowl of food. She furtively peeks through the screen door, not wanting to scare him away. He has to be the strangest looking cat she has ever seen, due to his unique markings. Her heart goes out to him in his hungry state. She notices that his tail curls, all black except for the white patch on the bottom, and that nose! She doesn't know why she thinks he's a boy, she just seems to know it.

In all these years she has never seen him before. He must have wandered into the neighborhood from the local dumpster, he is so filthy. Even in his disheveled state, she can see that he is still pretty young. Probably the by-product of an unwanted kitty union, one of the many forgotten creatures of this world. An orphan, just like me. Anne feels a chill run through her at that last thought, as the cat looks up and locks eyes with her.

He immediately springs into action, meowing and scratching at the screen door, trying to get to her. What harm could it do? She asks herself, this has always been a haven for cats after all. The new carpeting has just been installed, but if she keeps him on the front tiled entryway, she could let him in for just a minute. She tentatively pushes the screen door open and jumps back as the cat shoots forward like a rocket, leaping into her Mom's favorite chair, circling twice before curling into a ball and laying down.

Tears spring to Anne's eyes—she can almost see her mother sitting there, a cat in her lap and a glass of wine in her hand while watching Monday Night Football. The cat purrs loudly and looks up at her, his amber eyes shining. She reaches out and strokes his head as he kneads in delight, making himself completely at home, as only cats can do. If this isn't a sign, I don't know what is, she thinks as she catches a sudden whiff of her mother's favorite perfume. For the first time in what feels like an eternity, she is completely at peace." You're quite the independent little guy" she says to him, "I think I'll call you Indy."

The cat can't put it into words, he is a cat after all, but he instinctively knows that he belongs with them. He knows a cat person when he sees one, and the silver-haired lady with the kind face is definitely in his tribe. Every night he has heard her calling out to him "Here kitty, kitty!" from across a great distance and has been following her voice for days now, across many miles. He could see her inside, sitting in a chair behind the younger woman that he already knows as his new person. Jumping up onto her lap and receiving affection from both spiritual and earthly beings, as is his due, the cat is finally content. His new person will do fine just as long as she remembers to keep feeding him dinner.

Anne takes a final look at her childhood home, all freshly painted and cleaned out. This moment is bittersweet, but she knows it will be ok. She turns and locks the door. The real estate agent will begin the first showings in the morning, and they are confident it will sell right away. She bends down and picks up a freshly bathed Indy, tucking him under her arm as he purrs happily. Her husband is going to kill her, she thinks, but Indy will win him over, she loves him already. This is going to be the beginning of a beautiful friendship, kid, just like the old movie says. She gives him a quick kiss on the head before getting into the car and taking him to his new forever home.

The silver-haired lady watches as they drive away, satisfied that her final task has been completed. She backs away from the front window as the curtain gently settles back into place as if moved by an invisible breeze. Those two are a match made in heaven, and I know my daughter will be ok. With heaven on her mind, she takes her leave of this world, excited and ready for her new adventure to begin.

The Christmas Cat Art Show
(Christmas 2016)
Mark Hudson

There is a place in Chicago that a couple
of ladies my friend Chris and I know that have
been holding art shows. It is called Empirical Brewery,
and it is a bar in Chicago, that is family-friendly,
and even dog-friendly! It is in a working-class
neighborhood in Chicago, and a lot of people
are dog-owners, so they bring their dogs to
this bar with them, and their kids!

The first show they had was an autumn-
themed art show. Jessica and Marcy
put it together. But even then, they were already
planning ahead for Christmas. They told me at
the Autumn Art show that the theme for the
Christmas show would be cats.

Apparently, the reason for the show was
to raise money for an orphanage for abandoned cats
(Totally sounds like something Grey Wolfe would do!)
who had been abused, or were disabled. My friend
Chris, or his mother perhaps, owns a cat that may
have had an abusive owner previously. Some
of my friends have strong feelings about people
who are mean to animals. One woman at the
show, who I believe was in charge of the
orphanage where we were raising money for
said she'd taken in twelve abused cats, and
took them in, nurturing them back into a trusting
relationship with humans!

My friend Chris and I went out for pizza
beforehand, because they don't normally serve
any food at the bar. But when we got there, Marcy,
the one who had been to a nearby restaurant,
a Middle-Eastern restaurant, (Lebanese) told
them they were having an art opening, and
they gave her a bunch of food for free! My
friend Chris and I barely had any room for
food after that pizza, but Marcy sent us home
with some delicious leftovers!

The art was all fantastic, and each
creation was unique in its own way. Marcy
said she had to do her paintings in one
day, and she felt she had to rush them,
and they weren't very good. I told her,
"No, they're amazing!" They were cats
with Christmas ornaments in the background.
She probably thought I was just saying
that to say that, but tons of other
people complimented her work too.

My friend Chris and I sat in the
back and drew, something we usually do.
I managed to draw two scenes of the
people there, and it captured the mood
of the event. Chris's back was to the three
pieces he contributed to the show, and
a couple was looking at his work, and
the man had hair died purple or red,
and a ring in his eyebrow. I said
a silent prayer in my head to God
that they would buy his piece, and
they did!

I'd say that this cat show had
a better vibe than the autumn show. The
autumn show was "anything autumn"
so most people did Halloween, and
there seemed to be a dark element.
But the Christmas show seemed more
upbeat, and another lady also sold a
piece. People just seemed happy,
and that's what the holidays should be.

A pet can make their owner happy.
I suppose that a pet can be depressed, too.
I can tell with Chris's cat, for instance,
it has emotional scars from its original
owner. When earlier that day I came
over to his house, the cat looked at
me in fear. Chris had to say, "No
he's a friend, it's okay."

It just goes to show how the way
we treat animals or people can have a
long-lasting effect. If we treat pets and
people with respect, they will think
of us that way. The show will go
through New Years, and some of
the proceeds go to the cat orphanage.
To a non-cat lover, it might not seem
like that important of a cause. But where
I live they have a big thing they
promote, "Black lives matter."
I agree, and I saw something
interesting on the train the other day.
There was an Asian man who had
a "black lives matter" button on,
and sitting across from him was
a black man who was smiling!

I do agree with that,
and I believe that all life that
God creates matters. It says
in the good book that God
even cares when a sparrow falls.
Then, my friend, imagine how
he must care for you, dear reader!

The Katz' Kittens
Sherry Williams

"Hand me down those bowls, please, dear," Mrs. Katz asks her husband.

Mr. Katz stretches his paws up to the top shelf and takes down the two neatly stacked bowls. He wraps his tail around his wife's and rubs his tabby cheek against her calico one as he hands them over.

"Thank you," she purrs, giggling lightly. "Oh, that tickles."

He purrs back at her and quickly licks her whiskers before turning to grab the milk from the refrigerator. He knows that makes the fur behind her ears bristle.

"Oh, you," she growls playfully as he pours the milk into the bowls.

She puts the casserole dish on the table and watches as her husband whiffs the air.

"Squirrel," he sighs pleasurably. "It must be a special evening."

She wraps her tail around his shoulders and purrs in his ear. "Every evening is special when we're together."

He turns his head and licks her fluffy cheek. She quickly licks his ear in that spot that makes his tail curl then pulls away. She sits at the table and pats the seat beside her with her long, sleek tail.

He joins her, and they twirl their tails together as they both put their heads in the dish and begin tearing the squirrel apart.

"Mm, that's tasty," Mr. Katz purrs as he rips off another piece. He dunks this bite in his milk.

Mrs. Katz leans in to lick a stray drop of milk from his whiskers.

He picks up a chunk of squirrel on his claw and holds it out for her. As she stretches to bite it, he pulls it quickly away and gives her whiskers a solid lick.

She snarls and growls, snapping her teeth at him.

"Uh oh," he laughs. "Am I in the dog house now?"

With gleaming eyes, he holds out his squirrel-covered claw again and purrs as she grabs the meat with her teeth.

Slowly and teasingly they work together to devour their meal and put the mess away.

Mr. Katz licks Mrs. Katz' whiskers again then turns to walk to the living room.

Mrs. Katz watches him walk then gives a loud purr and leaps across the room, landing squarely on his back!

They tumble together, tails over paws, until they finally come to a stop, breathing heavily, with Mr. Katz pinned down by his shoulders.

"Cheeky," he purrs at his wife, stretching his neck to rub their whiskers together.

They both begin purring and walk together to their pillow to groom each other.

The following week, Mr. and Mrs. Katz settle in to watch their favorite television show, "That Cat's Got Talent," and Mrs. Katz picks up her knitting.

"You're humming," Mr. Katz says.

"Oh, was I?" Mrs. Katz answers absently. "I do so love this yarn."

He wraps his tail around her shoulders and asks, "What are you making?"

"A sweater," she purrs softly.

"A sweater? Is your fur not keeping you warm enough?" Mr. Katz asks.

"It's not for me," she replies, wrapping her tail around his.

"Oh," he touches he whiskers with his. "Who's it for, then?"

"The kittens," she tells him.

He twitches his whiskers and perks up his ears at that.

"Whose kittens?" he asks.

"Yours," she says, yellow eyes gleaming.

"Oh, darling, do you mean it?" he licks her cheek excitedly.

"Mm-hm," she hums.

His ears flatten against his head, and his breathing comes faster and heavier.

"What's wrong?" Mrs. Katz notices her husband's distress and doesn't understand.

"We aren't ready for kittens!" he pants.

"Oh, don't be silly," she laughs at him.

"But it's so much responsibility," he cries.

"Posh!" she says. "It will be fine. You'll see."

"Oh, darling," he exhales into her ear.

She buries her nose in his neck and inhales deeply. "Yum," she says. "You smell like salmon."

"Mm," he purrs back. "Salmon sounds good. Shall we have dinner?"

She puts her knitting away, and they go to the kitchen to make dinner together. They leave the television on so they can hear the performers while they work. They'll eat in the living room tonight.

Mrs. Katz takes the bowls and milk jug to the living room and pours them out on the portable tv trays. Mr. Katz retrieves some salmon fillets from the refrigerator and shreds them with his claws. He puts the pieces on two plates, making sure Mrs. Katz gets the larger share and carries them to the living room.

He sets the plates on the trays then takes his seat. Mrs. Katz looks at both plates.

"What?" her husband says with a mouth full of salmon.

"You're wonderful," she purrs, wrapping her tail around his.

In response he picks up a chunk of salmon on his claw and pops it into his mouth, scraping his claw clean on his gleaming teeth.

She giggles and shakes her head at his antics, turning her attention to her own meal and their show.

By the time she finishes her salmon and milk, Mrs. Katz is yawning widely.

"Oh, goodness," she says through the yawn.

Mr. Katz pets her head with his tail, purring affectionately. "Go to bed, my dear," he says, allowing his whiskers to tickle her ear.

She licks his ear and heads off to bed. Within three turns around the pillow, she is fast asleep.

After watching his favorite detective movie where the clever cat detective captures his arch-nemesis, the Great Dane jewel thief, Mr. Katz joins his wife on their pillow. He buries his face deep in her chest and lets out a contented sigh. She gives a deep purr and curls around him without waking.

In the morning Mrs. Katz awakens to the smell of fried mouse. The morning sunlight streams through the window warming her orange and white fur. She stretches her forelegs, flexing her claws.

"Oh, you're awake," Mr. Katz meows.

"Good morning, love," Mrs. Katz smiles sleepily at him. "What time is it?"

"Breakfast time," he tells her with a grin.

"Mm, I thought I smelled mouse," she purrs.

She joins her husband, and they walk, tail-in-tail, to the dining room.

He serves her breakfast and nuzzles his nose into her neck while she eats.

"I have a surprise for you," his breath tickles her ear.

She purrs with a small laugh. "Mouse for breakfast AND a surprise? Oh my, you've been busy!"

"I certainly have. Thank you for noticing, Mrs. Katz," he teases.

She finishes her mouse, has a few laps of milk and purrs at him. "So, what's this surprise you've been working on?"

"Follow me," he licks her ear and walks away, tail held high in the air.

She shakes her head with a small smile, wondering at his silly romanticism. She follows him out the back door, across the garden, and to the tree line.

"What are you up to?" she meows in bewilderment.

"Over here," he says. "It's just right here."

Her eyes grow wide, and her whiskers twitch when she sees it.

"Were you out all night?" she asks, astonished.

"No, no," he assures her. "Just woke up really early."

She laughs and gives him a head rub against his fluffy cheek before nosing around in her surprise. She pushes a few twigs around and finds a large amount of bird feathers from almost every kind of bird in the forest and some plant fiber from various greenery.

"Oh, it's lovely!" she purrs louder. "How many birds did you harvest?"

He wraps his tail around hers again and tells her, "I got a half dozen myself this morning."

"Oh! We'll eat well for the next couple of days!" she interrupts him.

He grins at her. "Yeah, anything you want. Anyway, some of the neighbors had some fresh, too, and when I told them we were nesting, they were more than happy to contribute."

She rubs her head against his again. "Should we start taking this inside?"

"Yes, of course"! Where would you like to set up your nest?" he asks then picks up a mouthful of twigs.

"Perhaps the corner closet in the bedroom?" she suggests. "It's quiet with just enough light."

She picks up some sticks and leads the way.

They drop their sticks by the closet door, and Mr. Katz says, "You pick your spot, and I'll go get another load of twigs."

She steps into the closet and lies down in several spots. This spot has too much light. That spot has too little. This spot is too warm, and that spot is drafty. She finally decides on that spot halfway behind the wall and half in the door. She begins dragging the twigs over and weaving them into a nest.

By the time Mr. Katz brings in his sixth load of sticks Mrs. Katz is working more slowly and breathing heavily. He wraps his tail around her shoulders and speaks softly. "Come along, my love. We don't have to finish this today. Let's have lunch and a rest."

She nuzzles into his embrace and nods her head with a sigh. "You're right. Is there any cardinal?"

"How about blue jay?" he offers.

"Okay," she's only mildly disappointed. She craves the gamey flavor of cardinal, not the stringy texture of jay.

"I'll find some next time I'm out. Now, you go see what's on tv," he licks her ear and watches her fur ruffle as the chill runs down her spine.

She settles into her comfortable chair and turns on a movie about a queen who can't decide which tom she wants to father her kittens. By the time Mr. Katz sets up her lunch tray for her, she is in a relaxed half-doze.

He licks her head and purrs, laughing, "I don't know why you watch these movies. Anyway, you've seen this one. She chooses..."

"Nat!" she interrupts him. "That's not the point."

"No?" he asks.

"No," she states firmly.

"Then what, do tell, is the point?" he asks.

"For some cats," she explains, "it's a fantasy. For others, it's a horror story."

Mr. Katz purrs loudly at that and laughs at her. "And for you?" he presses.

She sighs back. "For me, it's sad. That poor queen. If either of those toms truly loved her, she wouldn't be faced with such a decision."

"The way I love you?" he rubs his head into his wife's belly.

She licks his head and says, "Exactly."

He finishes serving their meal, and they eat while the drama unfolds on tv.

When he finishes his meal, he notices she has fallen asleep in her chair. He turns the volume down so no loud noises in the show will disturb her and takes their lunch dishes to the kitchen. He leaves her milk in case she wakes up thirsty. He then sets about bringing the rest of the sticks, feathers, and fluff into the bedroom so she can continue building her nest at her leisure.

It is some time later when Mrs. Katz wakes up and realizes Mr. Katz is curled around her with his nose shoved deep into her chest. She moves her tail, so it lays across his shoulders and gives his head a lick. He opens his eyes and looks lovingly into hers.

"You fell asleep," she teases.

"Only following your example," he replies with a lick to her nose.

She purrs a small giggle and stretches her forelegs. She stands and arches her back.

"Oh, that feels nice," she meows pleasurably.

"I'll be right back," she runs her tail up his spine as she heads to the outside spot where she relieves herself.

When she's done, she goes straight to the bedroom to look at the supplies her loving husband has gathered for her nest.

"I thought you were coming back to watch another show," he softly scolds her.

"Oh! You scared me!" she yelps.

He purrs softly and smooths her fur with his tail. "Sorry," he chuckles.

"I'm already tiring quickly," she explains. "I want to get this ready while I can."

He licks her head again. "Whatever you think is best, love. There's still time."

"Yes," she agrees, "but it will go quickly."

The next two cycles of the moon do indeed pass quickly. Mr. Katz takes over all of the hunting and meal prep while Mrs. Katz prepares her nest and sleeps many more hours than usual. She grows healthy and fat, and Mr.

Katz falls in love with her all over again every day. He brings her any twigs, feathers, or fluff she requests for her nest.

"Oh," she groans as she turns to lie on her other side. "There must be a dozen kits in there. I'm always lying on one!"

"Lie on your back," Mr. Katz suggests, "and I'll groom your belly for you."

She rolls over and purrs her gratitude.

He begins licking her fur, helping her relax.

"A dozen, you say?" he asks softly.

"I'm big enough for it," she grunts.

"Oh, I don't know," he says. "Have you ever seen a queen who had a litter of a dozen? I bet you have five or six, tops."

"Ugh," she groans again and throws a foreleg over her face. "Then they must each be as large as a rat!"

He chuckles softly and continues grooming his wife until she begins to snore. He continues grooming some spots she's had a hard time reaching lately, but gently so as not to disturb her slumber. He falls asleep with his tail draped over her belly and his nose deep in her neck.

Mr. Katz wakes up to the sounds of his wife whimpering.

"My dear, are you alright?" he asks, concerned.

"Ooh," she cries. "Can't get comfortable."

"Poor love," he commiserates." Is it almost time?"

She's so tired her head barely lifts as she answers.

"I don't know. I hope so."

"Would you like some milk? Or fish?" he asks, desperate to help his beloved wife.

She groans at the thought. "No," she says. "I just want to rest."

"Can I help you to your nest?" he rubs his nose across her neck.

"Yes, help me up," she concedes after a moment's thought.

He helps her rise slowly and holds her to him with his tail as she laboriously hobbles across the room to the closet. At long last she climbs into the basket and collapses, panting heavily.

"Will you be okay by yourself for a few minutes?" He is worried about leaving her alone but must have a quick bite and a trip to relieve himself.

She grunts slightly. "I'm not going anywhere," she promises.

"I'll be back in a jiff," he kisses her neck and trots off to tend to his morning needs.

As he steps outside to relieve himself, their neighbor Miss Fluff sees him and walks over.

"How is dear Mrs. Katz?" the elderly queen asks.

"She just took to her nest this morning," he calls out, barely slowing down. "I have to get right back to her!"

"Why, I should say so!" Miss Fluff admonishes him.

"I'll be by with a robin casserole in the next few days."

"Thank you," he says as he rushes past again, this time headed into the house.

He grabs a blue jay out of the fridge and rips off two quick bites before going back to his wife's nest. She looks at him without lifting her head. He licks her forehead and puts his tail between her forepaws.

"I think the first one is coming," she pants uncomfortably.

"Go on, love," he encourages her. "Anything you need, I'm here for you."

She blinks her gratitude and love and bears down until the first kit pops out. Now the pain has passed she's able to breathe more steadily. Mr. Katz gently picks up the newborn and hands it to his wife for cleaning. He waits, wide-eyed and anxious, for her to speak.

"It's a tom!" she finally tells him.

"We have a kitten!" he says in awe. "You're a mommy!"

The pains overtake her before she can reply.

"Ooh," she groans. "Here comes the next one."

This second kit slides into the feathers and Mr. Katz gently hands it to its mother for cleaning.

"It's a queen!" she cries joyfully.

Five more times she has the birthing pains. By sunset, she delivers an additional three toms and two queens.

When the last one arrives, Mr. Katz cries out sorrowfully, "Oh no! It's a runt! And it doesn't look very healthy." He hands it to its mother, so she can see if there's anything to be done.

"It's another queen," she tells him. "But I don't know if she'll make it. I need to keep her warm."

The four toms and two healthy queens have already found teats and are nursing heartily. Mrs. Katz helps the runt find a teat, but it doesn't latch on. She is scared for this smallest of her kits.

"Would you like some milk?" Mr. Katz asks.

She looks gratefully at her husband and says, "Yes, please."

He rubs his whiskers against hers and goes to bring her a bowl of milk and a few bites of cardinal. By the time he returns the runt has already died. Mrs. Katz is holding the still-cooling little body, crying quietly, while the six surviving kits continue to feed.

Mr. Katz licks each kitten on the back then presses his nose into his wife's neck and cries with her. He wraps his tail around his family. After a moment he pulls back and sets the bird meat and bowl of milk in the nest.

"I'll take care of her in the morning," he says.

She raises her head and takes a few laps of the milk then grabs a piece of cardinal on her claw. She puts her head back down and sighs contentedly. "Mm, cardinal. I love a good, juicy cardinal." He smiles at her and licks her head while she cleans the meat off her claw.

She falls asleep listening to her husband purr and feeling her newborn kittens kneading at her full belly. She wakes up in the morning with her husband standing guard over the mewling kits.

When he realizes she's watching him he purrs and tells her, "I think we have our paws full with this litter. Especially this little calico queen. She's already reminding me of you!"

Mrs. Katz purrs at him and lovingly swipes her tail across his nose.

"Here," she says, finally letting the runt out of her embrace. "It's time to say goodbye to this one." She licks the dead kit one more time and allows her husband to take it away.

He carries it to the tree-line and begins digging a hole. Miss Fluff approaches, carrying a casserole.

"Oh dear, what happened?" she asks, dismayed.

"Four toms, two queens, and a runt," he tells her by way of explanation.

"Oh, the poor little thing," the elderly queen tuts. "Did it suffer long?"

"No, it didn't even feed. he is grateful for the small favor.

"And how is Mrs. Katz?" Miss Fluff asks.

"Recovering nicely. Would you like to come in?" he invites.

"Oh, if it wouldn't be an intrusion," she says. "And here's the casserole I promised."

"Thank you so much. Now, do come meet the kits."

"What a lovely nest! And the kits are just precious!" Miss Fluff coos.

Mrs. Katz rolls her eyes at her husband.

"I brought you a dish of my robin casserole," she tells Mrs. Katz.

"That's quite kind. Thank you," she answers.

"Not at all. Not at all," the elder says. "Do you need more feathers to spruce up your nest? I have quite a few collected."

"That's very generous," Mr. Katz replies, "but I've been collecting, too. I'll just get this cleaned up and refreshed in a bit."

Mrs. Katz yawns, perhaps a bit theatrically, and Miss Fluff takes the hint.

"Well, I'll just mosey along now and let you rest. I'm just up the road if you need anything. Anything at all, dear," she bids them a good day.

Mr. Katz sees Miss Fluff out then returns to his wife to begin the business of turning six newborn kittens into a family.

The Tell-Tale Tail
Claudia R. Coleman

"What is this thing called tail, Mother?" asked the Manx kit,

Seeing his betailed playmates walk deftly across a narrow strip of garden sunlight while

Describing strange symbols with that mysterious appendage.

"Don't worry about it," mom mewed, casting a sideward glance atailward.

"One doesn't need it!"

"But, Mother, the indignity!" the babe countered in a baleful whine,

"When to cross with any grace at all the narrow twig or banded branch,

Not to mention the wind-blown shadow on the garden path,

That very extension seems to be the *sine qua non*!"

"Tails are the mark of the *hoi polloi*, my tail-less sweet,"

Momma mewed." They're riff-raff all!

We're better off without such common extensions as a tail!"

"Perhaps it's a coding device, Mother. Could that be it?

The betailed ones have a language all their own

That keeps me at bay, out of the loop, high and dry!"

Junior meowed with mouth agape and ears laid back.

"Aye, code it is, you can be sure.

But it telegraphs their every emotion, their most sneaky intent.

We tail-less ones are not so unclever!

Our untailed tales keep our secrets tight.

Your dorsal cowlick can betray no plan,

No strategy of attack or counter," Mother said, her left arm aloft.

"We sans-tailed ones can easily feint and parry, with nary an effort."

"Mother, dear!" said the babe, amazed.

"Such skill and panache. Such flair and *élan*!"

"*Merci*, my untailed sweet," momma purred.

Then she assumed a boxer's pose.

"We can fight inside or out, jab and hook, stick and move without our opponent... that is, playmate reading our plan."

"I see, I see! No tell-tale tail betrays our guileful stratagem.

Why, Mother, you could have a career in the ring!"

Said the mom cat's fluffy dumpling.

"You are too kind, my all-ball one," momma purred.

"Now, let there be no end to your understanding of this:

We have the gift of no-tail,

We never stand in a queue of high swirling arms waving uselessly about.

For no tall tail tells our tales.

We have our way endlessly.

And the coda to our story forever remains unread."

Tiger
Patricia Walkow

The young girl never gave you a name.

Your magnificence in tawny gold, black, and white made a name unnecessary. She simply called you "Tiger" throughout her entire childhood. To this day, you are still Tiger.

She has never forgotten you.

You were the first one she ran to visit whenever she went to the zoo. Do you remember her?

She stood outside your cage and talked to you, asking you how you were and if they were feeding you well. Her hair was brown, and she had bangs.

Your enclosure was small. You were huge—a Bengal tiger, male, regal, probably insane.

The routine of your day pained your visitor. You took two steps then turned and took two steps the other way. That was your world. There was no room for you.

You always knew it, but now you know your visitor acknowledged it also.

As she left your cage to visit the seals in their pond at the top of the hill, she would often look back at you, still incarcerated in your cage, as though you had committed a heinous crime.

Two steps, turn... two steps, turn... two steps, turn...

How could you *not* have lost your mind?

You peered into the girl's eyes every time she visited. Even when you paced back and forth, your eyes focused on her face. Her eyes followed you. Do you remember her eyes? Did you know *your* eyes haunted her?

She worried about you. Were you aware she understood you should be free?

Just as you were the first one she visited each time she came to the zoo, you were also the last one she stopped to see before she left. She didn't even consider you an animal.

You were Tiger.

For twenty years the girl visited you. For twenty years your routine didn't change—it couldn't; the zoo staff never moved you to a larger cage.

Two steps, turn, two steps, turn, two steps, turn...

Before the girl moved away, she visited you once more. You had been part of her life for a long time.

At the zoo, she saw you were gone.

She was not disappointed. Her preference was your death over continued imprisonment. At least in the hereafter, you could be true to your nature again, and you were too splendid not to have an afterlife.

Zoos had changed since she was a girl. Animals were given more "natural" enclosures, with room to roam and climb. She wondered if you were in such a place, or if death was still more humane.

She needed to know.

As she passed your former cage, now empty, she was haunted by your image from all those years.

Two steps, turn... two steps, turn... two steps, turn...

Two steps, turn... two steps, turn... two steps, turn...

Two steps, turn... two steps, turn... two steps, turn...

She paced it out for herself. With her puny gait, compared to yours, it was five steps, turn... five steps, turn... five steps, turn... five steps, turn...

How did you do it all those years, Tiger?

She found a zookeeper and asked about you.

You had been sent to a game preserve, a place where people are caged in moving vehicles as they watch the animals live in a quasi-wild state. They weren't sure you could adjust. But you did, she was told.

The girl breathed a sigh of relief for you.

****

When she was a grown woman, the young girl who loved you had the opportunity to visit a shelter for large cats. The resident tigers were animals people tried to own as pets but gave up. Did they not know you can never truly own a tiger?

These rescued tigers now had a refuge in the mountains with a certain amount of room to roam within an enclosure of many acres. They were accustomed to people, but they were still wild. One of them reminded her of you, but he was younger than you would have been at the time.

During a visit to perform some volunteer work at the tiger sanctuary, the now-grown woman had the opportunity to get close to a tiger—not *you*, Tiger, but one of your distant kin. The keeper brought the tiger to her, and she ran her hand along the length of his majestic frame, surprised by the softness of his fur, terrified by his size, awed by his presence, and grateful he accommodated her need. She felt the life within his chest as he breathed in and out.

The tiger could not know she stroked his beautiful fur for you.

Yes... you, Tiger.

Traveling Tales
Beth Clegg

There were times it felt like I'd been homeless forever, especially when warm summer days became cold fall evenings. Never an "insider," I slept with one eye open. I must've been really tired that night I was awakened from a sound sleep, pulled from my shed-bed, stuffed in a box, and taken on a long car ride. We stopped, but the engine kept running as I tumbled from side to side before the box was tossed under a bush. I'll never know what I did, nor will I ever forget the terror that engulfed me.

Shaking more from fear than cold, I pushed the top open and dashed into an unknown neighborhood where I crossed a female's marked territory. It was nice to know there was another cat, but we'd never be friends. Felines are territorial and dislike sharing. Littermates are different. I even have a few friends who aren't related and get along, but they were kittens that grew up together.

A canine scent caused my back to arch. I'm wary of dogs. That doesn't mean I don't like them, they're just so yappy and boisterous. And that tail? Short or long, it never stops moving. Then another scent interrupted my reverie and brought me to a full stop. Claws extended. Back arched to the hilt. Ears flattened. But it was just another unfamiliar scent bombarding my senses. With a sigh of relief, I continued my search for a safe haven.

****

I settled into a routine. I found mice on a somewhat regular basis and slept in a tool shed. I avoided homes with smoke coming from a chimney after I jumped on a window ledge one day. A cat was curled up on a rug close to blazing logs in a fireplace. At least she was warm. I hate to admit wondering why it couldn't be me. I had to stop being negative, but it's difficult to be positive when your stomach's growling and you don't know where the next meal's coming from, or you're looking ahead while looking behind. You're always on guard, anticipating danger around every corner, never feeling safe, sneaking remnants of dried dog food that should've been discarded, or scratching through filthy garbage bins looking for anything edible. Hunger's made me cranky, but I'd never wish my life on another living being, feline or otherwise.

While walking the fence line one day I noticed a long-vacant house was now occupied by a woman and a cat. The cat was a funny looking thing. It had no tail, but I knew it was a cat. I may not know a lot of things, but I know a cat when I see one. Was it okay? Or trapped? The person who'd betrayed me months ago had left me with distrust that had blinded me. No matter, I promised myself I'd find a way to look after that cat.

Days became weeks after that initial sighting. As I watched from my secret hiding place one morning, Bobtail, my name for the cat, slept on the woman's lap while her coat was brushed. What did that feel like? From Bobtail's facial expression, it must be wonderful. But, how could she be that trusting? It was as if she didn't know humans couldn't be trusted. I would spend more time watching for signs of trouble.

****

I thought I was invisible crouched under numerous tree branches covered with large leaves that draped the fence behind the woman's house. Thinking I'd found a safety zone from prying eyes, I took a catnap. I was wrong. I awoke to find the woman on the patio watching me. It was a crisp, clear day, ideal for having coffee outdoors. I hoped it was a onetime thing. It wasn't. By week's end, nothing had changed. I'm on the fence. She's on the patio drinking coffee. I had to devise another route to the woodpile, my favorite hunting spot or set a new speed record running the fence line.

After making it back and forth several days without incident, I was feeling pretty cocky and confident when I heard, "Here kitty, kitty. I have food. You must be hungry. Let's be friends." A friendship with Bobtail was a stretch, but this woman and I would never be friends. Then a breeze wafted a scent in my direction, bathing me in an aroma so strong it almost pulled me off the fence. Instead, I fled.

It didn't take long before hunger drove me back. She was still seated at the table. She plead with me. I ignored her. She left the bowl on the table, went inside and watched from a kitchen window. I scaled down, raced across the patio, jumped on the table, and devoured the food. With a full stomach for the first time in months, I retreated to the shed to ponder this new situation. I fell asleep before finding a solution.

The pattern was repeated for about a week. I returned. She called. I stayed on the fence. She left food. Watched from the kitchen window. As our war of wits escalated, I told myself I stayed on the fence, so she couldn't dash out and grab me. Truth be told, I was testing her. I never said felines can't be exasperating. It's in our DNA, but after that first day when I almost choked as I scarfed down food, I left the fence and ate my meal in a leisurely fashion. Our non-threating relationship might've continued forever if nasty weather hadn't intervened.

****

I'd seen rain many times, but nothing like this. The distant tool shed wasn't an option, so I hunkered down on the fence under branches, shivering, miserable, wondering if I'd survive the torrential onslaught, when she appeared on the patio, a windswept umbrella doing nothing to keep her dry. She called. I made a split-second decision, slid down the slick wooden surface, and raced across the patio. She grabbed me, juggling the umbrella as she held me close saying, "It's alright. You're safe now," as she ran for the house.

I've never been verbal, and now I couldn't quit talking. I knew she didn't understand a word I said. I didn't care. I was so grateful my yowls kept coming like the torrents of water battering the exterior walls and roof of her home. I'd never experienced anything like the hugs and soothing sound of her voice as she swaddled me in a thick towel before tending to her own needs. We were both soaked to the skin, but she didn't seem to care. Bobtail came to investigate and didn't hiss or growl as if she realized the woman had saved me from the nasty weather. I devoured the contents of the food bowl and drank clean water before reality set in. I was inside a house with a strange woman and an even stranger looking cat. What was I thinking? I panicked. Rain or not, I wanted out.

The sliding glass door was ajar. I dashed out. Shot back in. The weather had intensified. I was soaked. Again. My emotions were like a runaway rollercoaster. Outside meant being cold, drenched, hungry, and miserable. Inside meant being with a woman I didn't trust and a cat I didn't know. Inside was the price I'd pay if I wanted to be warm, have a dry coat, and full tummy. I'd just eaten. I was still starving. If I stayed inside, I'd have another meal. This was a one cat household. Would Bobtail accept me once she realized I'd be permanent? I didn't want to be abandoned again. Visions of that long-ago night flashed through my mind as the woman toweled me dry a second time, whispering words of encouragement. I was still trembling, but I was weakening. What could a few hours inside hurt? This would be an adventure. Tomorrow the rain might be a thing of the past.

I did better inside than anticipated, although the slightest noise had me wide awake. Unrelenting rain and remembering the events that put me here put me right back to sleep. After breakfast, I split. Ate and fled without so much as a thank you rub against her leg. The next day I was on the patio waiting for food. By weeks end I was a resident who found it far more enjoyable to view the fence from the kitchen window than being on it. I also had a name. Puddy Tat. She said my black and white markings reminded her of a cartoon character cat named Sylvester, whose buddy was Tweety Bird. I didn't care who they were. I just knew when she called her words were spoken with love.

If you think my name's funny wait until you learn Bobtail's. It's Pouncer Puss. The woman said it was the perfect name for the scrawny kitten who bounded through a pet door in another house in another city and claimed her heart. I had to agree. That cat pounces. A lot. When it became apparent I wasn't going away we engaged in a few skirmishes. Hissing backs arched, legs like stilts, my tail full as a brush cleaner while hers could only be described as a twitching, spinning nub. She became obsessed with my tail, and when I'm asleep, she grabs it, kicks it with hind feet, and disappears faster than greased lightning while dodging my half-hearted swats. After resolving issues that make contented cats, like who got first lap time, tummy rubbed, or chin scratched, we eat side by side, wait patiently to be brushed, snuggle up during lap time, and wash each other's face and ears.

****

There couldn't have been a happier cat on the planet until the morning the woman picked me up and placed me in a box with several small holes. She ignored my ear-splitting yowl as we drove off. This couldn't be happening. I'd trusted her. Now I was being betrayed. Again. I was heartbroken. My sharp claws only left scratch marks on interior walls and were worthless when I tried to force the top open. Terrified and trembling, I uttered a weak yowl when the car stopped. I loved this woman and Pouncer Puss who I'd never see again. Then it was like a miracle.

She removed the box and entered an office. My nose told me there were cats, dogs, and humans I didn't know. I went from morose to full alert in a nanosecond.

Next, strange hands lifted me from the box, placed me on a cold metal table, and began prodding and poking my body. Ears, eyes, mouth, and parts I saw no reason to be checked. My trembling continued, but there was something about these strangers' hands that was reassuring. After a couple of painless injections, we were on our way back home. The woman had tried to tell me everything would be alright, but my yowling had drowned her out.

I'm very fond of Pouncer Puss and my caregiver, my name for her. One of my biggest adjustments was responding to my given name. I'd just showed up when I heard the word "cat" because that's what I am. A cat who'll never know what I did to deserve this, nor will I ever be able to show my love and gratitude to my caregiver who stops what she's doing several times a day, picks me up and whispers, "I love you, Puddy Tat."

Venus the Calico Coat
Mark Hudson

Venus is a cat that is divided in half;
one-part orange, one part black.
A "Chimera" cat, a Calico kitty,
she is hardly a critter for you to pity.
The female has two X-Chromosomes;
so this is a cat that deserves two poems.
One eye is black, the other is green,
an internet queen from the year 2014.
A chimera is made of two embryos,
this is a cat that your neighbors would envy though.
Scientists first tried experiments on mice,
I guess they do that with genes they splice.
The cat has white spots on its chest and paws,
it looks like a present from Santa Claus!
The imagination couldn't produce such a figment;
that is what they get from mixing some pigment!
Is this an example of the scientists playing God?
It depends on your view of what is odd!
A pet can maybe have his genes altered,
but a cat is one who should never be haltered!
A cat will do whatever it wishes;
be careful if you also have tropical fishes!
A cat is independent, no need for a leash;
cats are free spirits, you'll never capisce!

Wally
Roseanne Trost

I was never particularly fond of cats. They seemed sneaky and not much fun. When visiting any friend with a cat, I always sat on the edge of my chair, fearing the feline might jump on me.

Then Wally came into my life. I did not seek him out. He found my husband and me. Before I knew his name, I often saw him in our cul de sac. Birds dive bombed him. Wally just sat there.

One morning, I looked out the front door, and there he was, sitting as if he lived here. When I tried to shoo him away, he just looked at me, not moving. Later, I carefully opened the door, so he would not dart into the house, and gave him a bowl of milk. He looked at the bowl, at me, and closed his eyes. The milk was untouched.

Days later, I met his owner, a neighbor down the street. She introduced herself, "Wally seems to like your house. I see him on your lawn all day long. We now have two other cats. Wally is fed up. He barely comes home to eat. He's fifteen years old and has no time for all of this." She offered me a bag of cat food." Just in case you want to feed him." I reluctantly took it.

So, I began putting out food and water for Wally. He still scared me a bit. Once he got into the house, and I chased him out with a broom. No animals in my house.

The changes came gradually.

On a chilly, rainy night, Wally was huddled by our front door. Somehow, my husband got him into our garage and put towels together for a bed, which Wally avoided like it was on fire. When we peeked out during the night, he was sleeping in the makeshift bed, even snoring.

I bought a cat bed, cute matching food and water bowls, and a toy mouse. Wally was not into toys. The bowls were too nice for the garage, so he began dining in our kitchen.

Through the next months, Wally was given a few more privileges. We watched television together, but he was not invited to sit on the furniture. That would come later.

Wally, with little effort, won over our hearts. When his (other) owner put her house up for sale, she asked if we wanted to keep Wally. She was afraid he would go out and get lost in his new neighborhood. We were thrilled. Actually, we had been dreading the move.

It was so sweet to see Wally sitting in the driveway when I came home from work. I wondered if he sat there all day, or timed it for my arrival. I knew other neighbors fed him during the day, but he would follow me into the house and wait for dinner.

The week following 9/11, my husband left on an international business trip. Alone, I watched the telethon for victims and sobbed. My dear, sweet cat came over by me and placed himself across my feet. I knew he sensed my grief. By the end of the program, Wally was sitting on my lap, providing me comfort. I was so grateful for him. That night, he slept at the foot of my bed.

We have so many Wally stories.

Anytime there was a thunderstorm, he would dart into the house, and hide under our bed, his tail visible. Only a clap of thunder would cause Wally to move fast.

Once a big dog tried to charge him. I froze and feared the worst. Without moving, Wally hissed, and the dog backed off, whimpering.

On occasion, I turned on loud music and picked him up to dance with me. Wrestling out of my arms, he always headed for the door, desperately wanting to escape.

Wally started failing. He ate and drank very little. The vet asked if I wanted to try injections to make him more comfortable. Every morning, before leaving for work, I gave him a shot, worried that he might not make it through the day. Mostly, he stayed inside and did not seem to miss wandering the neighborhood.

One of the last times that he did venture outside, I spotted him at the end of our block. He was staring down into a water drain. Was he going to slip down the drain to die? Panicked, I called the vet.

She examined him and suggested it was time to let him go.

I held Wally in my arms, my husband next to me. We talked soothingly to him, tears running down our cheeks. After he was put to sleep, we sat there a while holding him, full of such sadness.

All these years later, we still recall how much joy he brought into our home, and laugh at his quirky ways.

We still miss him.

Wildcat
C.R. Beideman

I.

She careened along the lemon-scented hardwood before leaping out the cat door. The stillness of home's interior vanished; everything outside came alive—the swaying trees and the clouds morphing in warm, breathy wind were like an organism. She padded the worn dirt patches under the swings to the shaded grass under the slide, climbed the knotty rope netting to the deck and bounded a ladder to the jungle gym's crow's nest. With her tawny, svelte body tucked inside, her ears and eyes peaked above the brim. Her tag linted like a spyglass: Mouser, it read.

Daily she'd watch over the property, ever since she saw the large black shadow emerge from the forest and reach toward the kids. In the backyard, where only a notched wood fence barred the wilderness beyond, ravens were gathered in crab apple trees, diving, and pecking worms after morning rain. She'd deal with them. Though, it seemed all of a sudden pressing—in the breeze and sun, eyelids lulled by twinkling and swaying leaves—to take a brief nap.

Fear startled her awake. The backyard was clear, she saw. The fear was in her gut. It was in her dream. Below, the kids played in the grass. They lacked economy of movement. No grace, lame prey, but what they lacked in refinement was redoubled in devotion. Suddenly the ravens took squawking flight, and as a cloud shaded the yard, the air chilled. With her fur on end, Mouser ran a perimeter before heading inside to complete her interrupted nap. Warm milk would help.

Nature called. She exited the cat door at dusk and munched long grass. A vole skittered out. She lowered her head, and she bounded after it. The vole stopped, hiding in its own stillness. This tactic worked. Mouser studied it, pawed it, but the vole didn't move. When she swiveled her head to check on the crab apple trees, the vole resumed fleeing and was flattened. She batted its remaining life with more boredom than amusement. She'd make a gift of it.

Dozy morning lingered as Mouser lay purring on the bed and then the kids screamed. Mom and Dad threw up the blankets, launching Mouser. She landed on the carpet, wondering whether her routine had been so interrupted that stretching wasn't now an option. Mom consoled her white-faced kids. Dad flushed the batted vole discovered in a slipper. Mouser's tail bobbed as she passed the kid's bedroom.

At breakfast, her customary tuna was withheld. Mouser silently protested, barely touching her kibble, and went outside. She ignored the ravens, passed the crab apple trees and sat upon the fence. Its rough-cut beams still held bark in places. Beyond the backyard, the forest rustled. It called with many voices: insect, bird, and wind. She sniffed the air for an hour, went to her crow's nest atop the jungle gym, and napped until dusk. She awoke to find the kids below her on the swings. Rested, she stretched and checked for ravens. Finding none, she glanced at the back fence. The black shadow seemed to leak from the woods. Mouser leaped down and pawed the kid's socks. They carried her in the house, and she sharpened her claws until bed.

As a kitten, she'd played with the kids, chasing their toys. She'd purred and purred. Outdoors came later. The forest was still foreign territory.

****

As winter approached and each day was snuffed earlier than the last, the shadow began to take form. Always in peripheral vision, Mouser glimpsed a four-legged stride at the forest edge.

Smoke rose from the chimney, and soft light glowed in the windows. Cold air closed the doors, and tonight the kids played inside. But in protest of lost daytime, Mouser stayed out well after dark, waiting for the shadow. She listened to silence until a branch snapped. The sound echoed in her mind, and the shadow entered the backyard. Mouser's fur lifted, but she didn't budge. It lurked among the crab apple trees, then moved back the way it came. As it left, Mouser felt the forest thrumming in her rib cage. The home's warm light, the food and water and litter and love— in her curiosity she left them all to follow the shadow. As she stalked, sometimes it eluded her, never holding in one place. Then, in the rising moonlight, it coalesced into a great dark bear.

When Mouser chased it, the bear gamed. Once, it sat and waited for her, but up close it turned out to be a wet boulder. There it would be again, deeper into the forest, always retreating. Silver moonlight silhouetted the trees, and where the moon didn't touch, darkness hollowed the forest. Finally, Mouser thought she had the bear cornered, but she found only a cavity from a fallen cedar, roots tentacled in black contrast to moonlit rocks. Defeated and glancing back, the home's soft window light shown evasively; as she moved it blinked like a star through wispy clouds. Suddenly the bear walked beside her; it had no smell, and it startled her. This time it moved with slow, purposeful steps. She followed with caution that relaxed into a natural stalk as the bear led her into a deep ravine along a black-surfaced river that roared with a million mingled voices. She followed until dawn. As daylight gave depth and contrast to the forest, as though it were not merely illuminated, but ever materializing and dissipating, the bear vanished.

II.

A rodent tittered through a carpet of ocher leaves. Mouser pounced, and its tail tickled her whiskers as it slid down. She padded toward the river and looked past her reflection into a still pool, where minnows scattered. She pawed the surface. Her vision seemed to scatter, and she drank. Padding the river's edge, her alert eyes absorbed the immediacy of the forest, of the wild. Along the banks and up the ravine were boulder fields; the ravine was an endless jungle gym.

Mouser climbed and leaped from boulder to boulder, sniffing wonderful things, until a shadow circled. It sailed silent over the ocher carpet, and it grew. Mouser remembered the ravens. She heard the heavy beat of a wing, and her back spasmed with pain. Her body stretched and turned instinctively to attack, eagle talons cutting as she squirmed. With sharpened claws, Mouser swat the eagle near the eyes. A wing dipped and dragged on the earth, wreathing the pair in leaves. Mouser's caterwaul rose to the canopy, but her swat forced the eagle to release its grip. She landed and rolled until her claws found purchase in the earth. With a loud beat, the eagle gained elevation, screeched and was gone. Shivering, Mouser slid into a nook between two boulders.

Blood matted her fur. She smelled the bed of yellow and orange leaves. She felt overdue for rest, sedated. Through blurred vision the bear approached, its fur was blueish black in the sun; fanning in the breeze, each strand seemed alive. So ancient were its movements that it looked childlike—raising its snout and wiggling its nose, stopping to press against a burned cedar, up-ending it, licking grubs and termites. Mouser watched until her eyes darkened and closed but the bear roared, waking her, and it led her back to the river where it plunged in, wading neck-deep out to the middle. Finally, it submerged, and black oil lay in its place on the surface, swirling downstream. Instead of drinking, this time Mouser entered the cold mountain water, where her fur washed clean and her wounds clotted. She suffered into a huckleberry thicket, groomed and slept.

She dreamed the smell of cut grass and the soft texture of milk until a splash called Mouser out to play.

Waking from deep sleep, at first, she did not know where she was; before she could remember, she saw that across the river, another cat shook out its fur. The temporary mist held a rainbow. Concealed, Mouser studied the cat—black-tipped ears like mischievous horns, a silverfish dancing between its fangs. The bobcat settled in a deer bed to eat. Mouser was enchanted by her wild cousin, and afraid.

She sneaked away, following the river's gash until the boulder-strewn rapids hushed into deep emerald pools. As the river quieted, bird song rang in the canopy high above. She left the bank, carefully padded among the rocks and found shelter in a nook roomy enough for stretching. The clatter of burrowing rodents was nearly constant, and with the promise of hunting, she felt safe. For Mouser, shelter and food were always one muddled feeling.

****

Her memory of the bobcat lingered. As the days passed, her torn fur grew back, but against the grain. Voles and crayfish sustained her, and the birdsong slowly faded. Daily, she descended to the river, lapping water, listening for another splash, hoping for a chance to see the bobcat.

As muffling snow fell she lapped the almost ice surface of the river. An interesting smell was on the air. She felt her fur stand and quickly turned to face the bobcat, who wore his winter coat like a king. He fixed his eyes on her collar, on its unnatural chime. She meowed. He growled and passed her by and took a place on the river's edge, sitting tall and still. She hid, studying him. He'd grown since she first saw him, having eaten his share of fish. She wondered why he ignored the land: why didn't he, with his large paws and powerful haunches, bound after every snowshoe hair? Economy of movement, she realized. Watching him not flick a whisker, she knew he would never forget how to survive, and she wanted to learn.

Mute and stoic, the bobcat fished until his tail began to hover and wind. Almost imperceptibly, his statue head lowered as if becoming too heavy to lift. Then it happened so fast she had to replay it in her mind afterward: fat snowflakes fell on the water as his paw lifted. Yellow eyes unblinking, his breath rippled on the surface. Claws sliced through the stillness and plunged shoulder deep. One paw met the other while his body drew out like a weasel, his stout hind holding firm to the bank. Emerging from his plunge, he held the fish between his paws. The tail flapped. It flapped as he consumed the silverfish.

****

Mouser and the bobcat mirrored each other on opposing banks. She wondered where he crossed the river; he covered a much larger range. Snow accumulated on their whiskers and between their ears. It gathered on the golden eagle above, and on the heron in the cattail. Like a reflex, when one creature broke the stillness, shaking off their white lumps, the others would too. No one out fished the patient spear-beaked heron, and Mouser was thinning. She never fished long, distracted by tittering rodents in their labyrinths beneath the snow. She'd punch through with her forepaws, bounding and disturbing the fishers. But voles were unfulfilling meals.

She perched tall over a divot in the bank with still and clear water beneath her. A sucker fish hovered in view.

She lowered her head to the surface, ignoring her reflection. Suddenly she loosed her claws. Her foreleg numbed instantly as she thrust it into the pool. The fish was slippery. She tried to pincer it with the other paw and fell in, but with this leverage she pressed it into the mud, calming the fish, and increasing her grip. She bit hard into the fish's side and surfaced, fur matted to her frame. She lifted her chin and tilted her head to keep the flapping fish aloft, and she trot away from the bank to a secluded spot like she'd seen the bobcat do. She let if flop as she shook off and lick dried. The eagle and heron flew off. The bobcat moved upriver. She enjoyed the eyeballs best.

III.

High up the ravine chasing grouse, Mouser dashed into the woods as the truck's chains clanked up the switchback logging road. Curious, she followed until the driver cut the engine. In the open, the biting wind bore into her ears. Snow muffled the man's step down from his truck. Snow immediately clung to his wool hat and coat. He rubbed his hands together, then he retrieved a rifle from behind his seat, and slung it diagonally on his back. He rubbed his hands together again and opened the tailgate. Two hounds leaped out, running inefficiently, sniffing madly. She descended to her stone den in the rock pile along the river.

Her bed was matted grass, leaves, and clumps of moss. Despite subzero weather, her den felt warmer with a solid base of snow around it. It smelled earthy and pungent compared to the vacant, untouched air outside her den. It was too cold to fish—they gathered in the deepest holes in the middle of the river. Even the vole tunnel network was silent. The encounter with dogs made her restless, so she went down to the river. The emerald basins were iced over, and only a thin slice of fast water remained where otter were buoying up to spot danger. They suddenly disappeared beneath the surface, and Mouser slunk away from the riverbank. A canyon rending blast preceded the bobcat, who approached Mouser from downriver. His ears were high and faced out, his eyes were frantic. Hidden in a thicket, she meowed. He looked at her in surprise and his pace increased. He moved upriver, thrumming lowly. She followed. She ran to keep up. He serpentined boulders and scree as the ravine filled with the urgent yelp of hounds. He bounded up toward a burned ridge in great leaps. She proceeded at a cautious stalk. The ravine steepened and funneled into a narrow gash lined with spires of ice. Howls rushed up after the cats, reverberating in the choke. Pillows of snow *whumphed* down from unseen heights. Mouser clawed up the very ice and perched on a shelf in time to see the bobcat top out. The two hounds wailed, impeded by drifted snow. Frothing, they plowed a path to the ridge. The hunter did not reveal himself. When the hounds passed under her, she leaped down the ice spire and followed them, moving easily in their wake. Topping the ridge, she watched them taking turns trying to run up a lofty fir.

The bobcat was treed.

Mouser saw the hunter now. His legs punched through the snow to his hips. His flannel chest heaved. When he removed his hat to wipe sweat, steam rose from his head. He used all fours at times. Mouser clawed up a fir's charcoal trunk where she could see the bobcat. She meowed to him, and he roared back. The hunter leaned against a tree, breathing heavily. He took off his mittens. Mouser's stomach lining burned, and her claws dug deeper into the tree. The dogs were ceaseless, throats hoarse, screeching, mad for blood. They silenced at the gun's crack. As the bobcat fell, snow-muffled its fall.

The man strapped the steaming bobcat to his back and wandered over the burned ridge toward the logging road, usurping a kingly coat. From her high perch, Mouser saw a shaft of sunlight pierce the gray sky, illuminating a far off, tawny field.

****

Snow pitted and browned, the river swelled, but the sun-scorned ravine moved too slowly into spring, and Mouser abandoned her winter den. The land was golden in the valley beyond, where bison moved in little earthquakes, and Mouser sped the flat ground full bore instead of precise bounds among rocks. She chased a pocket gopher along the barbed wire fence line. She pounced as it dove into a hole near a post, and she snagged. Her collar caught and dragged a wire bail. She pulled until the bail caught on the fence, jerking her back. Her collar choked. She panicked and thrashed until her breath grew short, and her eyes grew dim. Remembering the bobcat and his grace even in death, she resigned, allowing the collar to take her weight. The bear appeared on the horizon, silhouetted by the half sun falling over the edge. It played with the sun like a big orange ball, as if determined to pop it. Mouser calmed and found a reserve of strength. Instead of thrashing, she turned and tried to back out of her collar. Again, and again, she yanked her head, and finally, she shook like she had a fish and slipped her collar. Her tags chimed with faded memories of comfort and love and then were silent.

Crossing the bison field, Mouser strode toward the big orange ball. It fell over the back of a forest, which she entered. Through muddled gloam, she saw a light blink like a star through wispy clouds. As the woods thickened, she lost the light, but she heard music, and curiosity drew her. She padded across a whispering creek on a fallen log, and the light reappeared. From behind a boulder, she peered out. A human stood before flame, its shadow projected high and stark against a cedar stand. Mouser smelled smoke, and she hid. The gun had smoked. But the music called.

****

The camper didn't notice the cat, not consciously. It lurked on the periphery of his vision. His ancestral genes sensed the presence, but he wasn't attuned to them. He scrubbed his cookware, rinsed his dirty fingers and dried them on his beard. He sat in a sack-bottomed camp chair, gazed into the bonfire, and fished a harmonica from his pocket. He crossed one foot over his knee and tapped the beat with his other. The harmonica tasted like copper; it felt electric in his teeth when he played.

He paused. There it was again. This time he noticed it. He realized that he *had* noticed it the first time: eyes, little glowing eyes. He clicked his headlamp and walked in front of the fire, scanning low among the tree trunks, and saw nothing. But when he resumed his music, a cat approached. It had been watching, he knew. It sat tall-backed across the fire from him. Was it wild? But it was too small. But it was nine deep in the backcountry. Fire fanned between him and the cat, who meowed. He lowered his hand, rubbing his thumb and fingers together like he held food.

"Here, kitty."

He blinked, and she was gone.

A NON-PROFIT EDUCATIONAL SANCTUARY

Big Cat Rescue

Big Cat Rescue is one of the largest accredited sanctuaries in the world dedicated to abused and abandoned big cats. They are home to about 80+ lions, tigers, bobcats, cougars, and other species—most of whom have been abandoned, abused, orphaned, saved from being turned into fur coats, or retired from performing acts.

What sets Big Cat Rescue apart is that they are working to end the abuse at its root by ending the private possession and trade in exotic cats through legislation and education. The sanctuary began rescuing exotic cats in November 1992.

Big Cat Rescue's mission is to provide the best home they can for the cats in their care, end abuse of big cats in captivity, and prevent extinction of big cats in the wild.

https://bigcatrescue.org/

~ 150 ~   Write To Meow 2017

www.ingramcontent.com/pod-product-compliance
Lightning Source LLC
Chambersburg PA
CBHW051042030426
42339CB00006B/153